Dynamically Downscaled Climate Simulations over North America: Methods, Evaluation, and Supporting Documentation for Users

By S.W Hostetler, U.S. Geological Survey; and J.R. Alder and A.M. Allan, Oregon State University

Open-File Report 2011–1238

U.S. Department of the Interior
U.S. Geological Survey

U.S. Department of the Interior
KEN SALAZAR, Secretary

U.S. Geological Survey
Marcia K. McNutt, Director

U.S. Geological Survey, Reston, Virginia: 2011

For more information on the USGS—the Federal source for science about the Earth, its natural resources, natural hazards, and the environment—visit http://www.usgs.gov or call 1–888–ASK–USGS.

For an overview of USGS information products, including maps, imagery, and publications, visit http://www.usgs.gov/pubprod.

To order this and other USGS information products, visit http://store.usgs.gov.

Suggested citation:
Hostetler, S.W., Alder, J.R. and Allan, A.M., 2011, Dynamically downscaled climate simulations over North America: Methods, evaluation and supporting documentation for users: U.S. Geological Survey Open-File Report 2011-1238, 64 p.

Contents

Figures

Tables

Conversion Factors

Multiply	By	To obtain
Length		
millimeter (mm)	0.03937	inch (in.)
meter (m)	3.281	foot (ft)
kilometer (km)	0.6214	mile (mi)
Mass		
kilogram (kg)	2.2	pound (lb)
Area		
square meter (m^2)	10.76	square foot (ft^2)
square kilometer (km^2)	0.3861	square mile (mi^2)
Flow rate		
millimeter per day (mm d^{-1})	3.281	foot per minute (ft/min)
meters per second (m s^{-1})	2.236	feet per second (ft/sec)
cubic meters per second (m^3 s^{-1})	35.314	cubic feet per second (ft^3/sec)
Pressure		
Pascal (Pa)	0.01	millibar (mb)
hectopascal (hPa)	1.0	millibar (mb)
Energy		
Watt per square meter (Wm^{-2})	0.000088055	BTU per second per square foot (BTU sec^{-1} ft^{-2})

Temperature in degrees Celsius (°C) may be converted to degrees Fahrenheit (°F) as follows:
°F=(1.8×°C)+32
Temperature in degrees Fahrenheit (°F) may be converted to degrees Celsius (°C) as follows:
°C=(°F-32)/1.8

Dynamically Downscaled Climate Simulations over North America: Methods, Evaluation, and Supporting Documentation for Users

By S.W Hostetler[1], J.R. Alder[2], and A.M. Allan[3]

Abstract

We have completed an array of high-resolution simulations of present and future climate over Western North America (WNA) and Eastern North America (ENA) by dynamically downscaling global climate simulations using a regional climate model, RegCM3. The simulations are intended to provide long time series of internally consistent surface and atmospheric variables for use in climate-related research. In addition to providing high-resolution weather and climate data for the past, present, and future, we have developed an integrated data flow and methodology for processing, summarizing, viewing, and delivering the climate datasets to a wide range of potential users. Our simulations were run over 50- and 15-kilometer model grids in an attempt to capture more of the climatic detail associated with processes such as topographic forcing than can be captured by general circulation models (GCMs). The simulations were run using output from four GCMs. All simulations span the present (for example, 1968–1999), common periods of the future (2040–2069), and two simulations continuously cover 2010–2099. The trace-gas concentrations in our simulations were the same as those of the GCMs: the IPCC 20th century time series for 1968–1999 and the A2 time series for simulations of the future. We demonstrate that RegCM3 is capable of producing present-day annual and seasonal climatologies of air temperature and precipitation that are in good agreement with observations. Important features of the high-resolution climatology of temperature, precipitation, snow water equivalent (SWE), and soil moisture are consistently reproduced in all model runs over WNA and ENA. The simulations provide a potential range of future climate change for selected decades and display common patterns of the direction and magnitude of changes. As expected, there are some model-to-model differences that limit interpretability and give rise to uncertainties. Here, we provide background information about the GCMs and the RegCM3, a basic evaluation of the model output and examples of simulated future climate. We also provide information needed to access the web applications for visualizing and downloading the data, and give complete metadata that describe the variables in the datasets.

[1]U.S. Geological Survey, Department of Geosciences, Oregon State University, Corvallis, OR 97331, USA
[2]College of Oceanic and Atmospheric Sciences, Oregon State University, Corvallis, OR 97331, USA
[3]College of Oceanic and Atmospheric Sciences and Department of Geosciences, Oregon State University, Corvallis, OR 97331, USA

Introduction and Background

Widespread interest in understanding past, present, and future climate change and variability and the response and feedbacks of natural and managed ecosystems has motivated the development and application of models and techniques to provide climate data at relevant spatial and temporal scales. A wealth of observational data is available to support research over the historical record and geologic records provide indirect evidence of climate changes in the past. Quantitative estimates of paleo- and future climate (including atmospheric circulation as well as surface-climate variables), however, must be obtained from climate models that account for the interactive changes in the global atmosphere and oceans that are driven by global boundary conditions, such as atmospheric trace-gas concentrations and aerosols, earth-sun geometry, sea ice, sea level, and continental ice sheets. Simulations of global climate are conducted with general circulation models (GCMs), which are designed to balance model resolution and physics with computational requirements and limitations. Hence, long climate simulations (for example, centuries to millennia) have necessarily been run at relatively coarse spatial resolutions, which are on the order of a few degrees in latitude and longitude. GCMs are now being run for shorter time periods at finer resolution; however, the prevailing approach for obtaining finer spatial resolution climate information is to apply techniques for downscaling GCM output (for example, Maraun and others, 2010).

Downscaling techniques fall into two very different categories: statistical and dynamical. The techniques are complementary and both have strengths and weaknesses (table 1). Many variations of statistical downscaling exist, ranging in complexity from simple interpolation to application of statistical neural networks and weather generators. Wilby and others (2004) and references therein provide an excellent introduction to and overview of the techniques. All techniques are applied to downscale the climate (for example, temperature and precipitation) of a GCM grid cell (order of hundreds of kilometers in latitude and longitude) to a high resolution grid (order of ten kilometers or less). The high resolution grids are based on digital elevation models (DEMs) that represent more realistic topography than can be represented by low resolution GCMs.

Downscaling techniques can be relatively uncomplicated. For example, differences or anomalies between a future period and the present are calculated for each GCM grid cell, the anomalies are interpolated to a high resolution grid and the differences are added to observed climatology on the same high resolution grid (for example, Tabor and Williams, 2010). An additional computation is usually employed for precipitation to scale modeled values so the changes are essentially converted to percent change that is consistent with observed values. More complex techniques involve building statistical (for example, regression) relationships between observed climate fields and the grid cells of the DEM (for example, between 500 hPa heights and precipitation, Cayan and others, 2008). For temperature-related variables, the GCM data for the present and future are interpolated to the high resolution grid using these relationships and temperature lapse rate corrections. Various methods are used for distributing precipitation to reflect more realistic topography and to conserve the total precipitation from the GCM. The relatively smooth fields from the GCM are thus distributed to a grid that more realistically represents finer scale topography. There is limited ability to compensate for features in the GCM, such as orographic precipitation over mountainous regions that can be displaced geographically due to smoothed topography.

Dynamical downscaling or regional climate modeling (RCM) also relies on output from GCM simulations. Output from GCM simulations is used to derive time-varying (for example, 6-hour) lateral (vertical profiles of temperature, humidity, wind) and surface (pressure and sea surface temperature) boundary conditions for a three-dimensional model domain that is selected to capture the important synoptic- and mesoscale atmospheric circulation features that determine the climatology of a region of interest. The 6-hour boundary conditions are assimilated along the four edges and surface (ocean) of the model domain and the RCM then simulates atmospheric circulation and surface interactions internally. We illustrate "nesting" of an RCM in a GCM with maps of upper level pressure height and winds, sea level pressure and winds and surface temperature and precipitation for August 1996 (fig. 1). (The figures in this report are at 300 dpi resolution to limit the size of the file. The original figures that were created at 600 dpi resolution are available for download. See appendix A for details on accessing the electronic versions of the figures in this report.)

The nesting technique provides a high level of fidelity between the synoptic-scale GCM fields and the associated mesoscale resolution fields simulated by the RCM. The time sequence of the maps in this example illustrates the building of a blocking high pressure cell at 500 hPa and an associated heat-induced surface low pressure cell over the Great Basin, a common summertime feature. The associated temperature and precipitation maps display warm temperatures over the Great Basin and a well-developed monsoon over the Southwest that extends into the inter-mountain West. At present, nesting of the RCMs within GCMs occurs only in one direction—from the GCM to the RCM—so there is no feedback between the models. Two-way nesting techniques, in which a GCM and an embedded RCM interact continuously, are being developed at a number of modeling centers. One-way nesting is potentially subject to mismatches between the simulated fields and those of the GCM along the exit or downwind boundary of the RCM. Such mismatches occur, for example, because the amount of water vapor or the wind speed in the RCM differs from that of the GCM, which can result in excessive precipitation along the boundary. For this reason, model domains are usually designed to be larger than the area of interest so that a number of grid cells can be trimmed away from the border to eliminate boundary artifacts.

To a large extent, the climate variability of the driving GCM determines the variability of the climate produced by the RCM. Although regional climate models in general can improve on the details of GCM simulations through dynamical downscaling over complex terrain, they cannot, for example, improve upon or make substantial changes to features of the large-scale circulation or SSTs produced by a GCM. This means that, for example, if the jet stream is incorrectly placed in a GCM, it also will be incorrectly placed in the RCM. Regional climate simulations thus reflect not only model-to-model differences among the driving GCMs but also added internal biases related to parameterization of physical processes (for example, cloud formation) and other factors. It is known, for example, that the choice of the numerical scheme that is used in RegCM3 to simulate convective precipitation influences other fields, such as air temperature.

Purpose

This report documents a suite of simulations of present and future regional climate that we produced for research applications. The climate simulations were run with the regional climate model, RegCM3, which is a high resolution atmospheric model coupled to a physically based model of surface processes (the BATS, Biosphere-Atmosphere Transfer Scheme). The overarching goals of the modeling project were (1) to assess the feasibility of producing high resolution (50- and 15-km) simulations over North America, (2) to provide high resolution weather and climate data for the past, present, and future, and (3) to develop an integrated data flow and methodology for processing, summarizing, viewing, and delivering the climate datasets to a wide range of potential users. Here, we provide basic information and discuss the 15-km simulations for Western North America (WNA) and Eastern North America (ENA). The discussion is limited to basic validation of the annual and seasonal averages of simulated temperature and precipitation, mapping, and comparing seasonal averages of simulated temperature, precipitation, snow cover, and soil moisture as simulated by the models, and mapping future changes in these fields for 2020–2029, 2040–2049, 2060–2069, and 2090–2099. We prescribed atmospheric composition in the RegCM3 simulations to match the 20th century and A2 scenario time series that were developed for the IPCC AR4 (Intergovernmental Panel on Climate Change, 2007) and used in the driving GCMs. We selected the A2 scenario because it provides an upper bound on future emissions and because it is similar to the RCP8.5 scenario developed for the IPCC AR5. Trace-gas concentrations are updated in the regional model on an annual basis.

In a parallel and ongoing effort, we are developing web-based tools that allow users to visualize and download our model datasets. The web applications, which have been developed with inputs and feedback from managers and colleagues, distill a large volume of climate model data to provide visualization of a few key climate variables, such as air temperature, precipitation, snowpack, and growing degree days at national, state, and county levels and over telescoping hydrologic units or HUCs (Seaber and others, 1987). A variety of temporal resolutions (for example, monthly and decadal) allow users to investigate a range of potential change over meaningful geographic areas. We also have developed fast, flexible, and comprehensive tools to extract and download data over user-selected areas and time frames. We will be adding additional future-climate downscaling products to our web applications and data base. We also will be adding ongoing dynamically downscaled simulations of paleoclimate that will span from the Last Glacial Maximum 21,000 years ago to present in 3,000 year increments. We provide information about the web applications and how to access the datasets in appendix A and we provide the metadata for the datasets in appendix B.

RegCM3 Description

RegCM3 is the third generation of the Regional Climate Model originally developed at the National Center for Atmospheric Research during the late 1980s and early 1990s. The model is supported by the Abdus Salam International Centre for Theoretical Physics (ICTP) in Trieste, Italy. Here, we provide an abbreviated description of the model.

RegCM3 is comprised of a dynamical core (Grell and others, 1995), physics representing radiative transfer (Kiehl and others, 1996), large-scale or dynamic precipitation (Pal and others, 2000), convective precipitation (Grell, 1993), a planetary boundary layer component (Holtslag and others, 1990; Holtslag and Boville, 1993), a biosphere component BATS (Dickinson and others, 1993), representation of open ocean (Dickinson and others,1993; Zeng and others, 1998) and closed water bodies (lakes) (Hostetler and Bartlein, 1990; Hostetler and others, 1993; Small and others, 1999) and atmospheric chemistry and aerosols (Qian and others, 2001). These components are coupled and interactive. Further details of these model components and application of the model can be found in numerous publications (for example, Giorgi and others, 2004a, 2004b, and references therein and Pal and others, 2007, and references therein), the ICTP RegCNET web site (http://users.ictp.it/RegCNET/model.html), and the ICTP RegCM publications web site (http://users.ictp.it/~pubregcm/RegCM3/pubs.htm).

RegCM3 requires time-dependent lateral (that is, vertical profiles of wind, temperature, and humidity) and surface [surface pressure and sea surface temperature (SST)] boundary conditions that are continuously updated every 6 hours of simulation. The lateral boundary conditions derived from GCM output are assimilated into the RegCM3 with exponential decay in space over 12 grid cells around the perimeter of the model domain. Boundary conditions for RCMs are derived by preprocessing saved GCM fields into a standard format that can be read into the model. Virtually all GCM history files differ both in their format and composition so it is necessary to develop specialized preprocessing codes to accommodate GCM-specific output.

Energy, water, and momentum are exchanged between the surface and atmosphere through the atmospheric boundary layer. The surface is represented by the BATS (Dickinson and others, 1993; appendix B, fig. 37) that simulates surface processes related to vegetation (for example, evapotranspiration, leaf temperature, and phenology) and hydrology (for example, soil moisture, runoff, and snow) that vary in response to atmospheric conditions. The soil zone in BATS has a depth of 3 m, which is subdivided into a 0.1 m surface layer and a vegetation-dependent root zone that ranges from 1 to 2 m. Soil moisture and soil temperature are computed. BATS thus provides a large set of variables that are either directly simulated by the model or that can be derived from model output (appendix B). BATS Surface types and their associated physical parameters are summarized in table 4.

Model Domains and Simulation Periods

Our climate simulations include six regions or model domains (fig. 2). The North American (NA) domain has a horizontal grid spacing of 50 km and 23 vertical levels, the Eastern North America (ENA) domain has a horizontal grid spacing of 15 km and 23 vertical levels and the Western North America (WNA) domain has a horizontal grid spacing of 15 km and 18 vertical levels. We found that it was necessary to divide the West into four overlapping domains in order to achieve the necessary balance between boundary forcing, regional dynamics and the quality of the simulations over the complex topography of the region. The model produced an unacceptable cold bias over a single, large WNA domain due to a combination of complex topography and the large horizontal distances from the center of the model to the GCM boundary forcing.

The 50-km simulations over the NA domain are intended to provide atmospheric and surface fields to allow analysis of large-scale circulation and modes of variability (for example, the Pacific–North American teleconnection, pattern, PNA) in the past, present, and future. The 15-km simulations provide high resolution of weather and surface fields that better reflect topographic forcing that dominates the West. Together, the 50- and 15-km simulations allow joint analysis of synoptic-scale circulation variations and the resulting surface responses.

We used output from four GCMs to derive boundary conditions for the RegCM3 (table 2, table 3, fig. 3). The NCEP RegCM3 simulation is driven by atmospheric and surface fields derived from the NCEP-NCAR Reanalysis project that is run by NOAA (Kistler and others, 2001). The reanalysis project assimilates a large array of observed atmospheric and surface data into the NOAA AGCM, which is run simultaneously to produce spatially and temporally continuous global datasets. The NCEP Reanalysis data thus provide a gridded, optimal estimate of climate variables that are constrained by observations (for example, temperature and precipitation). It is standard practice in regional climate modeling to use reanalysis products as driving boundary conditions because, in theory, the resulting RCM simulations should be in the best agreement with observations. Additionally, the NCEP simulations provide spatially and temporally complete and internally consistent gridded sets of climate and surface variables that can be used "off line" to calibrate process models.

Global climate simulations from the GFDL CM 2.0 and the MPI ECHAM5 were part of a suite of model output used in the Climate Model Inter-comparison Project (CMIP-3) and the IPCC AR4. Both GCMs have long development histories and have been widely applied to climate research. More information can be found on the CMIP-3 website (*http://www-pcmdi.llnl.gov/ipcc/model_documentation/ipcc_model_documentation.php*), IPCC Data Distribution Centre website (*http://www.ipcc-data.org*) and the web pages of the individual modeling centers. We gratefully acknowledge the individual modeling centers for providing the history files needed to derive boundary conditions for the RegCM3.

GENMOM (GMA2 in tables 2 and 3) is a recently developed GCM comprised of the GENESIS V3.0 atmospheric GCM and the MOM V2.0 oceanic GCM. Both component GCMs have been applied extensively to climate research. The model is relatively low resolution (T31, ~3.75° × 3.75°) by design, a compromise that allows long simulations to be made in reasonable time so that the model can be applied to paleoclimate and future experiments that commonly are run for multiple decades and centuries. GENMOM is not part of the CMIP-3 or CMIP-5 model evaluations. We are participating with GENMOM simulations in the Paleoclimate-Modelling Inter-comparison Project (PMIP), which is part of CMIP-5.

The GENMOM simulations of future climate were produced as an additional downscaled data set under the A2 emissions scenario. The A2 simulations are part of a larger data-model comparison effort aimed at evaluating the ability of our GCM and RCM to simulate North American climate and climatic variability in response to changes in global boundary conditions (for example, insolation, atmospheric composition, continental ice sheets, sea level, and paleogeography). The simulations span the last glacial maximum (LGM, 21,000 years ago) through the Holocene. Details and an evaluation of the GENMOM simulation of present-day climatology are given in Alder and others (2010).

Overview of General Circulation Models

To provide some background that is relevant to coupling GCMs with RCMs, we provide a brief overview and comparison of a representative group of GCMs that were used in the CMIP and IPCC AR4, including the models used for our regional climate simulations. We focus on summarizing simulated surface temperature and precipitation because these variables can be readily compared with observations and because the degree of agreement with observations and among the models is an indication of how biases in the GCM atmospheric circulation and sea surface temperatures may influence associated RCM simulations.

All GCMs are designed to simulate the dynamics and processes of the atmosphere and ocean; however, the models can differ in how the processes are represented or parameterized, the numerical methods used to solve model equations, the horizontal and vertical resolution at which the models are run and how the atmospheric and ocean models interact. These model-to-model differences translate into differences in the sensitivity of the individual models to changes in forcing (for example, volcanic eruptions and atmospheric trace-gas concentrations) and in their simulated climatologies.

The global distribution and gradients of mean-annual air temperature climatology simulated by the IPCC GCMs compare well both with observations and among the models (fig. 4). Relative to observations, model-dependent cold biases are evident over the Northern Hemisphere with a range of cold and warm bias over North America (fig. 5). The GFDL CM2.0 and GENMOM simulations display cold biases over North America of several degrees or more on an annually averaged basis.

Climate models simulate both dynamic precipitation (for example, wintertime storms moving off the North Pacific Ocean into the Pacific Northwest) and convective precipitation (for example, thunderstorms, the monsoon over the Southwest). The physics and the temporal and spatial characteristics of precipitation are complex. Improving the ability of models to simulate precipitation remains a major challenge and goal for climate modelers. The global patterns and gradients of precipitation are captured by the models, but not as well as those of air temperature (fig. 6). The observed precipitation maximum in the equatorial region is reproduced in general by the models, but the magnitude and distribution of the maxima vary considerably with respect to observations and among the models (fig. 7). Most of the models tend to produce too much precipitation over Western North America and too little over Eastern North America. This pattern is associated with sea surface temperatures and the mid- to high-latitude atmospheric circulation. The wet bias in GFDL CM2.0 and GENMOM precipitation over Western North America coincides with the cold bias discussed above.

A fundamental metric that is used to characterize climate models is their sensitivity to a doubling of atmospheric CO_2 ($2XCO_2$) concentrations. The average, global temperature sensitivity of the GCMs that are included in the IPCC AR4 is ~$3°C$, with a range of $2-4.5°C$. The temperature patterns simulated by models generally are similar globally (fig. 8). High-latitude warming (that is, "polar amplification") is a common feature in all simulations, as is a larger response of land as opposed to ocean temperatures. Regionally, the sensitivity of the models can differ by up to a few degrees (fig. 8). Although the general agreement among the models is remarkably good at the global scale, such regional difference in their sensitivity is a factor in determining temperature response changes at the regional scale. Over North America, the GCMs used to drive the RegCM3 display a range of sensitivities of $2-3°C$ (GENMOM), $2-4°C$ (ECHAM5), and $3-5°C$ (GFDL CM2.0).

Basic Evaluation of RegCM3 Simulations

We evaluate the ability of the RegCM3 to simulate the present-day climate with output from the runs that were driven with the NCEP Reanalysis fields. For the period(s) beginning in 1982, the NCEP Reanalysis I and II atmospheric fields and the weekly NOAA Optimum Interpolation Sea Surface Temperature (SST) V2 were used to create boundary conditions. To extend the runs back before 1982, the NCEP Reanalysis I and II atmospheric fields and the HadISST sea surface temperature (from the UK Met Office Hadley Centre for Climate Change) datasets were used to create boundary conditions. The driving NCEP fields are a combination of observations (for example, sea surface temperature) and simulations (for example, vertical profiles of temperature, wind, and humidity) and so there is some expected departure of simulated fields from observations where such observations exist. Nonetheless, the resulting RegCM3 simulations are, in theory, the highest quality that can be achieved under a given model configuration. Some degree of improvement in the RegCM3 simulations might be realized by tuning model parameters related, for example, to precipitation over specific regions but we chose to use the same model parameters for all regions. The only difference in the model configurations is the size of the domains and the number of vertical levels used to represent the atmosphere (18 for WNA, 23 for ENA).

The RegCM3 simulations are continuous simulations run over specified date ranges such as 1985–1999. Boundary condition files with a time step of 6 hours were created from the GCM history files and are used to force RegCM3. A frequency of 6 hours captures the diurnal cycle and dynamics of atmospheric flow in the GCM associated with features such as mid-latitude storms. The computational time step of RegCM3 for the 15-km simulations is 30 seconds; a small time step is required to ensure numerical stability of the model. The atmospheric model communicates with BATS every 180 modeled seconds. The size of the ENA domain limits the simulations to 2.5 modeled months per computational (wall-clock) day, although the smaller WNA domains allow about one model year per computational day using our current hardware configuration.

The raw data from the model are saved every 3 hours for the WNA domains. For the ENA simulations, surface fields are saved every 3 hours and the atmospheric and radiation fields are saved every 6 hours. The total volume of raw data from all simulations is now about 300 terabytes. The raw data from the simulations are post processed into monthly and daily files; the surface files contain 48 simulated and derived surface variables and three-dimensional atmospheric files contain 14 variables (appendix B).

Extensive evaluation of the fields for which observed data are available is a very large and time consuming task that involves acquiring and manipulating a variety of datasets; that effort is ongoing. Here, we provide a basic evaluation in which we compare simulated annual and seasonal average temperature and precipitation with the gridded PRISM data set (Daly and others, 1994). For the comparisons, we created a modified PRISM dataset by aggregating the standard 4-km dataset onto our 15-km model grids. The PRISM dataset is derived using a variety of statistical relationships and algorithms based on station data, and thus, has some limitations, particularly over high elevations where observations are lacking (Daly, 2006). In addition, the geographic extent of the PRISM dataset we used is limited to the conterminous United States, whereas our model domains cover much of North America. Our evaluation is in the form of differences or anomalies (modeled values minus PRISM values) that display the bias between the simulated values and the PRISM values. We calculated the differences at each model grid point and mapped the differences as averages over the Level III EPA Ecoregions. The Level III ecoregions provide a relatively small-scale aggregation that reflects the mountainous terrain of the West, and averaging within the ecoregions filters out the "noise" associated with the grid square-by-grid square variability of the anomalies. There are obviously numerous details both within and among the maps; here, we provide brief summary comments and we leave a more detailed evaluation to the reader.

Western North America

The overall ability of the model to reproduce observed air temperature over WNA on an annual and seasonal basis is quite good. Simulated annual average temperature bias generally is less than 2°C (fig. 9). Some of the apparent bias over higher mountainous areas may reflect the inherent topographic smoothing in the model or a lack of observed data and the comparatively simple method used to interpolate to high elevations in the PRISM data or both. Greater biases are evident in the seasonal averages, particularly during the spring (MAM); however, the overall seasonal bias also is typically less than 2°C.

Differences between simulated precipitation and the PRISM data are, as expected, more variable than the air temperature differences (fig. 10). As is the case with air temperature, a lack of high-elevation observations of precipitation influences the PRISM data; an additional potential complication with the PRISM precipitation data is that it is much more difficult to interpolate precipitation both horizontally and vertically from the observations (for example, Hewitson and Crane, 2005). In the PNW, a winter dry bias is simulated along the coast and a wet bias is simulated inland. A similar pattern occurs in the PSW domain. These discrepancies are in part attributed to underrepresentation of coastal mountains that control precipitation, even on the 15-km grid. Additional dry bias along the PNW coast is attributable to edge affects along the southern boundary of the model domain. Patterns of positive and negative bias are evident in annual precipitation over the NRM domain (fig. 10). Although the biases generally are small, they persist in all seasons, suggesting possible inaccuracies in the NCEP upper air circulation or problems with how the RegCM3 incorporates the circulation or both. The largest disagreement between simulated precipitation and the PRISM data is the dry bias along the southeastern part of the SRM domain (fig. 10). Elsewhere in the SRM domain, the biases are much smaller and similar to those of the other domains (fig. 10). The persistent dryness along the border suggests that the model domain may not cover a sufficiently large area of the Gulf of Mexico to capture the circulation that brings precipitation to that region. This may be particularly true with regard to large storm events (for example, hurricanes and tropical depressions) that are recorded in the PRISM data but not simulated effectively by RegCM3.

The four domains covering WNA overlap by 22 rows of latitude and 22 columns of longitude. In the final datasets, the first 12 rows and columns are trimmed from around the border of the domains to eliminate most of the edge effects where the driving GCM fields are introduced to the model. Thus, there are 10 rows and columns of overlap between adjacent domains in the trimmed fields. It is important to assess the fidelity of the simulations where the domains overlap to assure continuity among the regions. As an example, for orientation, the arrows in figure 9 point to the Middle Rockies ecoregion. The Middle Rockies is common to all four domains and is in proximity to the domain borders. The temperature biases in the Middle Rockies located within the four domains indicate that the annual and seasonal averages differ by less than 1°C (fig. 9). Similar concordance is exhibited in the precipitation biases where the magnitude of the differences generally is less than 0.5 mm d^{-1} (fig. 10). The Middle Rockies in the SRM domain displays a dry bias in the annual, MAM and JJA averages. The magnitude of the dry bias is less than -0.5 mm d^{-1} and the other three domains display a wet bias of less than 0.5 mm d^{-1}, indicating good agreement in the simulation of precipitation where the domains overlap.

9

Maps of seasonal averages for simulated air temperature, precipitation, snow-water equivalent and soil moisture for the NCEP, and the present-day ECHAM5, GFDL, and GMA2 simulations over WNA provide visual comparisons of the similarities in the spatial and temporal characteristics of the respective climatologies (figs. 11–14). The seasonal spatial patterns and gradients of the selected fields are reproduced in all simulations and domains, particularly where the coastlines and mountainous topography are strong influences on climate. The wet winter/dry summer seasonal cycle of the Mediterranean climate over the PNW is evident in all models (fig. 11) as is the Southwest monsoon (figs. 12–13). Differences are apparent among models in spatial patterns such as the eastward displacement of the Southwest monsoon in the GFDL simulation and in the magnitude of the variables such as the overly wet Southwestern monsoon in the ECH5 and GMA2 simulations or the snow water equivalent (SWE) values in the GFDL simulation that are consistently greater than those of the other three simulations.

Future Climate

We illustrate examples of future climate by mapping changes in the seasonal averages of the simulated air temperature, precipitation, snow-water equivalent and soil moisture (figs. 15–30). The decadal averages for 2020–2029, 2040–2049, 2060–2069, and 2090–2099 are compared to the 1985–1999 present day averages. The ECH5, GMA2, and GFDL RegCM3 simulations display a range of change both in magnitude and in the rate of change in the future. Changes in the simulated fields predominantly display similar trends and spatial patterns across models and domains; however, differences in the magnitude and the spatial patterns of the future changes are evident. The discrepancies are attributed to model-to-model differences in the atmospheric circulation and SSTs from the GCMs and the response of RegCM3 to incorporating the GCM forcing. Some of the fields display changes that are not unidirectional, particularly for the decades of the 2020s and 2040s before atmospheric trace gas forcing becomes stronger (for example, air temperature and SWE). Persistent patterns of change in the future are regionally wetter or drier reflecting persistent changes in atmospheric circulation. These regionally heterogeneous patterns may not be present in the low resolution GCM simulations of the future suggesting that the changes are attributable to high resolution topographic forcing of circulation by orography that is present in the regional model.

Eastern North America

We modeled ENA with one large domain and 23 vertical levels in an attempt to capture low-level atmospheric circulations associated with the Gulf of Mexico. ENA lacks the topographic complexity of WNA that acts to anchor atmospheric circulation and strongly influences climate in nature and in the model. Moreover, ENA is influenced by a wider range of seasonally varying atmospheric circulation patterns that interact in complex ways. Thus, in some ways, simulating the regional climate of ENA presents a bigger challenge than simulating the regional climate of WNA.

The annual and seasonal differences between the simulated and PRISM air temperatures are generally ±2°C or less, which is similar to WNA (fig. 31). The simulation is colder than PRISM in the Southeast during all seasons, particularly during summer. The differences between simulated and PRISM precipitation also generally are similar in magnitude to those of WNA (fig. 31). There is persistent dryness in the simulation over the Southeast and Gulf Coast regions. The large DJF dry bias along the Gulf coast present in the SRM simulation also is present in the ENA simulation. The seasonal patterns of temperature and precipitation biases suggest multiple explanations. The lack of precipitation in DJF indicates possible shortcomings in RegCM3 with the placement and strength of the Southerly jet stream, deficiencies in the NCEP forcing or SSTs, or some combination. Cool, dry biases in JJA along the Gulf and Southeast point to a lack of onshore wind flow at low and mid-levels that in turn is associated with misrepresentation of the strength and position of the semi-permanent Bermuda high pressure cell in either the NCEP boundary conditions or in the response of the RegCM3 or both. The widespread cool and dry biases in SON may reflect a failure of RegCM3 to simulate heavy precipitation events associated with tropical cyclones and hurricanes, both of which substantially influence the observed records. The model simulates frontal precipitation and convective storms that can deliver high-intensity rainfall events; however, as is the case for other regional climate models, RegCM3 has limited ability to simulate the intensity of the wind fields associated with large-scale cyclones and hurricanes and thus the precipitation and movement of such storms. The ability of global and regional climate models to simulate cyclones and hurricanes has advanced considerably in the past few years and there are now GCMs that use high-resolution nested grids (for example, the model developed by GFDL) and regional climate models [for example, the Weather Research and Forecasting model developed by NCAR (Skamarock and others, 2005)] that are capable of simulating the formation and dynamics of hurricanes. We will fully evaluate the cause of the dry, cool patterns in the model elsewhere; such an evaluation is beyond the scope of this report.

Maps of seasonal averages for simulated air temperature, precipitation, snow-water equivalent and soil moisture for the NCEP, and present-day ECH5, GFDL, and GMA2 simulations over ENA provide an adequate comparison of the similarities in the spatial and temporal characteristics of the respective simulations (fig. 32). As is the case for WNA, there are numerous details apparent in the maps and we provide only a very general and brief overview discussion. The seasonal spatial patterns and gradients of the selected fields are reproduced in all simulations. Differences in how the GCMs simulate seasonal SST patterns are evident (fig. 32). Relative to the NCEP simulation, GMA2, GFDL, and ECH5 reproduce the seasonal gradients of precipitation over the continent well but all produce excess precipitation over the Atlantic Ocean (fig. 32). Seasonal patterns of snow-water equivalent and soil moisture are consistent among the simulations (fig. 32)

Future Climate

We demonstrate examples of future climate over ENA by mapping changes in the seasonal averages for simulated air temperature, precipitation, snow-water equivalent and soil moisture domains (figs. 33–36). Where such data exist, simulated decadal averages for 2020–2029, 2040–2049, 2060–2069, and 2090–2099 are compared to their respective 1985–1999 present day averages. As is the case with WNA, the three RegCM3 simulations display a range and rate of change in the future. In general, the mapped changes in the simulated fields display similar trends and spatial patterns across models; however, differences in the magnitude and spatial distribution of the changes are evident and reflect differences in the atmospheric circulation and SSTs of the GCMs and the response of RegCM3 to the GCM forcing. Some of the fields display changes that are not unidirectional, particularly for the decades of the 2020s and 2040s before atmospheric trace gas forcing becomes stronger (for example, air temperature and SWE). It also is apparent that persistent patterns of change in the future (for example, precipitation) are regionally wetter and drier than present, reflecting changes in atmospheric circulation. The regionally wetter and drier conditions, for example, may not be present in the low resolution GCM simulations of the future suggesting that the changes are attributable to high resolution topographic forcing of circulation, internal bias in the RegCM3 originating from model physics, how the GCM forcing is incorporated, or a combination of the three.

11

Summary

This document provides basic information about our regional climate simulations for North America. We describe the regional climate model (RegCM3) and its implementation and application to simulate present and future climates of WNA and ENA on 15-kilometer model grids. This is the first attempt at simulating very high resolution, multi-decadal time series using the output from several different GCMs. We provide a range of possible future climate. Overall, the results are encouraging, but there are model-to-model differences that lead to uncertainties when comparing datasets. Nonetheless, our continuous datasets are internally consistent and they provide comprehensive time series of surface and atmospheric variables for further scientific research. Our web applications support visualization of the data to explore it in a variety of ways and they provide access for downloading partial or full datasets.

Disclaimer and Terms of Use

We have attempted to produce the highest quality model simulations based on sound experimental design and accurate processing of the model output. We have fixed any errors that we have found or that have been brought to our attention by collaborators; however, it is certain that some errors still exist. We caution that, as is the case with other climate models, there are limitations to the modeling approach and the simulations of the future actually represent climate sensitivity tests and not necessarily true projections.

All model datasets are freely available and are intended for further climate-related scientific research. Although these data have been processed successfully on a computer system at the U.S. Geological Survey (USGS), no warranty expressed or implied is made regarding the display or utility of the data on any other system, or for general or scientific purposes, nor shall the act of distribution constitute any such warranty. The USGS shall not be held liable for improper or incorrect use of the data described and/or contained herein.

Acknowledgments

This project was funded by the U.S. Geological Survey under the National Research Program, National Climate Change and Wildlife Science Center, the Climate Change Program, the Climate and Land Use Research and Development Program and the Northern Rockies Science Center. Additional funding was provided by the U.S. Fish and Wildlife Service through the Great Northern Land Conservation Cooperative and the Bureau of Land Management Rapid Ecosystem Assessment program. Our project would not have been possible without the very high level of computing support that was provided by the Environmental Computing Center of the College of Oceanic and Atmospheric Sciences, Oregon State University. We thank the Max Planck Institute for Meteorology, Hamburg, Germany, and the NOAA Geophysical Fluid Dynamics Laboratory, Princeton, NJ, for providing GCM history datasets. Over the course of this project, many colleagues and collaborators provided valuable feedback on documentation, design of the web applications and quality control of the datasets. We are grateful for their input, suggestions, and criticisms.

References Cited

Alder, J.R., Hostetler, S.W., and Pollard, D., 2010, Evaluation of a present-day climate simulation with a new atmosphere-ocean model, GENMOM, Geoscience Model Development, v. 3, p. 1697-1735. doi:10.5194/gmdd-3-1697-2010

Cayan, D.E., Maurer, Dettinger, M., Tyree, M., and Hayhoe, K., 2008, Climate change scenarios for the California region: Climatic Change, v. 87, p. 21-42.

Daly, C., 2006, Guidelines for assessing the suitability of spatial climate data sets: International Journal of Climatology, v. 26, p. 707-721.

Daly, C., Neilson, R.P., and Phillips, D.L., 1994, A statistical-topographic model for mapping climatological precipitation over mountainous terrain: Journal of Applied Meteorology v. 33, p. 140–158.

Dickinson, R., Henderson-Sellers, A., and Kennedy, P., 1993, Biosphere-atmosphere transfer scheme (BATS) version 1e as coupled to the NCAR community climate model: Technical report, National Center for Atmospheric Research, Boulder CO.

Giorgi, F., Bi, X., and Pal, J.S., 2004a, Mean, interannual variability and trends in a regional climate change experiment over Europe. I: Present-day climate (1961-1990): Climate Dynamics, v. 22, p. 733-756.

Giorgi, F., Bi, X., and Pal, J.S., 2004b, Mean, interannual variability and trends in a regional climate change experiment over Europe. II: Future climate (2070-2100), Climate Dynamics: v. 23, p. 839-858.

Grell, G.A., 1993, Prognostic evaluation of assumptions used by cumulus parameterizations, Monthly Weather Review, v. 121, p. 764-787.

Grell, G.A., Dudhia, J., and Stauffer, D.R., 1994, A description of the fifth-generation Penn State/NCAR mesoscale model (MM5). Tech. Note TN-398+IA, Technical report, National Center for Atmospheric Research, Boulder, Colorado.

Hewitson, B.C., and Crane, R.G., 2005, Gridded area-averaged daily precipitation via conditional interpolation: Journal of Climate, v. 18, p. 41-57, doi: 10.1175/JCLI3246.1.

Holtslag, A., and Boville, B., 1993, Local versus nonlocal boundary-layer diffusion in a global climate model: Journal of Climate, v. 6, p. 1825–1842.

Holtslag, A.A.M., de Bruijn, E.I.F., and Pan, H.L., 1990, A high resolution air mass transformation model for short-range weather forecasting: Monthly Weather Review, v. 118, p. 1561–1575.

Hostetler, S.W., and Bartlein, P.J., 1990, modeling climatically determined lake evaporation with application to simulating lake-level variations of Harney-Malheur Lake, Oregon: Water Resources Research, v. 26, p. 2603-2612.

Hostetler, S.W., Bates, G.T., and Giorgi, F., 1993, Coupling of a lake model with a regional climate model: Journal of Geophysical Research, v. 98(D3), p. 5045-5058.

Hostetler, S.W., Bartlein, P.J., and Holman, J.O., 2006, Atlas of climatic controls of wildfire in the Western United States: U.S. Geological Survey Scientific Investigations Report 2006-5139. (Also available at http://pubs.usgs.gov/sir/2006/5139.)

Intergovernmental Panel on Climate Change, 2007, Climate Change 2007: The Physical Science Basis. Contribution of Working Group I to the Fourth Assessment Report of the Intergovernmental Panel on Climate Change, Solomon, S., D. Qin, M. Manning, Z. Chen, M. Marquis, K.B. Averyt, M.Tignor and H.L. Miller (eds.), Cambridge University Press, Cambridge, United Kingdom and New York, NY, USA.

Kiehl, J., Hack, J., Bonan, G., Boville, B., Breigleb, B., Williamson, D., and Rasch, P., 1996, Description of the NCAR community climate model (ccm3): Technical Report NCAR/TN-420+STR, National Center for Atmospheric Research, Boulder, CO.

Kistler, R., Kalnay, E., Collins, W., Saha, S., White, G., Woollen, J., Chelliah, M., Ebisuzaki, W., Kanamitsu, M., Kousky, V., van den Dool, H., Jenne, R., and Fiorino, M., 2001, The NCEP-NCAR 50-year reanalysis: Monthly means CDROM and documentation: Bulletin of the American Meteorological Society, v. 82, p. 247-267.

Maraun, D., Wetterhall, F., Ireson, A.M., Chandler, R.E., Kendon, E.J., Widmann, M., Brienen, S., Rust, H.W., Sauter, T., Themessl, M., Venema, V.K.C., Chun, K.P., Goodess, C.M., Jones, R.G., Onof, C.M., Vrac, C., and Thiele-Eich, I., 2010, Precipitation downscaling under climate change: recent developments to bridge the gap between dynamical models and the end user: Reviews of Geophysics, v. 48, doi:10.1029/2009RG000314.

Pal, J.S., Giorgi, F., Bi, X., Elguindi, N., Solon, F., Gao, X., Rausher, S.A., Francisco, R., Zakey, A., Winter, J., Ashfaq, M., Syed, F.S., Bell, J.L, Diffenbaugh, N.S., Karmacharya, J., Konaré, A., Martinez, D., Da Rocha, R.P, Sloan, L.C., and Steiner, A.L., 2007, Regional climate modeling for the developing world, The ICTP RegCM3 and RegNET: Bulletin of the American Meteorological Society, v. 88, p. 1395, DOI:10.1175/BAMS-88-9-1395.

Pal, J.S., Small., E.E., and Eltahir, A.B., 2000, Simulation of regional-scale water and energy budgets: Representation of subgrid cloud and precipitation processes within RegCM, Journal of Geophysical Research, v. 105(D24), p. 29,579-29,594.

Pan, Z.-T., Takle, E., Segal, M., and Arritt, R., 1999, Simulation of potential impacts of man-made land use changes on U.S. summer climate under various synoptic regimes: Journal of Geophysical Research, v. 104, p. 6515–6528.

Qian, Y., Giorgi, F., and Huang, Y., 2001, Regional simulation of anthropogenic sulfur over east Asia and its sensitivity to model parameters: Tellus, v. 53, p. 171–191.

Seaber, P.R., Kapios, F.P., and Knapp, G.L., 1987, Hydrologic unit maps: U.S. Geological Survey Water Supply Paper 2294, 66 p. (Also available at http://pubs.usgs.gov/wsp/wsp2294/html/pdf.html.)

Skamarock, W.C., Klemp, J.B., Dudhia, J., Gill, D.O., Barker, D., Wang, W., and Powers, J.G., 2005, A description of the Advanced Research WRF version 2: NCAR Tech. Note TN-468+STR, 88 p.

Small, E.E., Sloan, L.C., Hostetler, S.W., and Giorgi, F., 1999, Simulating the water balance of the Aral Sea with a coupled climate-lake model: Journal of Geophysical Research, v. 104(D6), p. 6583-6602.

Tabor, K., and Williams, J.W., 2010, Globally downscaled climate projections for assessing the conservation impacts of climate change: Ecological Applications, v. 20, no. 2, p. 554-565.

Wilby, R.L., Charles, S.P., Zorita, E., Timbal, B., Whetton, P., and Mearns, L.O., 2004, Guidelines for use of climate scenarios developed from statistical downscaling techniques: Supporting material of the Intergovernmental Panel on Climate Change, DDC of IPCC, 27 p., accessed August 30, 2011, at http://ipcc-ddc.cru.uea.ac.uk/.

Zeng, X., Zhao, M., and Dickinson, R.E., 1998, Intercomparison of bulk aerodynamic algorithms for the computation of sea surface fluxes using TOGA core and TAO data: Journal of Climate, v. 11, p. 2628–2644.

Appendix A. Web Applications and Data Access

We are currently providing web-based tools to visualize and download the monthly surface variables described in appendix B. We are processing daily values for the surface variables and monthly and daily values for the 3-dimensional atmospheric variables listed in appendix B. We will release these additional datasets in the future. Two visualization tools are available that allow users to interrogate and evaluate the data. We provide averages and aggregates of selected key variables in the datasets over a variety of spatially delineated polygons including states and counties and HUC codes 4-8. The third web-based tool can be used both to visualize and download the data. The tool makes use of a number of software packages that are integrated into one user environment. The tool is relatively advanced and requires some effort and experimentation by users to become familiar with the wide range of options and settings that are included. Finally, the complete monthly data sets may be downloaded via ftp from our server. Monthly files for the four WNA domains are 44.2 megabytes per year and files for ENA are 123.6 megabytes per year. Files downloaded via the web application are time series for each variable for the duration of the simulation (for example, monthly average air temperature for 1968–2099) and are much smaller than the full monthly files.

Access to Data Website

With the exception of the tutorials, which use comma-separated-variable (CSV) format, the downloaded datasets are currently provided in netCDF format only. The data are geographically registered on the Lambert Conformal projections that are used by the RegCM3. Projection information is written in the metadata of each file. The file formats are compatible with most netCDF viewers such as Panoply (free software for a variety of operating systems available at *http://www.giss.nasa.gov/tools/panoply/*) and they can be imported directly into software packages such as ArcGIS (v9.3 and higher), R and Ferret. The visualization tools may be accessed by following links at USGS/GNLCC web page: *http://regclim.coas.oregonstate.edu*. The web page includes information from this report and additional background information. Changes, additions, and modifications to the datasets will be updated and posted as they occur.

Monthly data files are currently being served by a Thredds Data Server, which provides data access via OPeNDAP, NetCDF Subset, direct link and also provides WMS mapping. OPeNDAP provides a mechanism to stream data directly into analysis applications such as Matlab, IDL, Ferret and IDV without downloading the entire dataset. Both OPeNDAP and NetCDF Subset allow datasets to be subdivided by variable, time, and space so that only the data of interest is downloaded, which greatly reduces the time to download and the storage required to download datasets. Access to the Thredds data catalog can be found at: *http://regclim.coas.oregonstate.edu:8080/thredds*.

The netCDF files that include all variables may be downloaded from via anonymous ftp from: *regclim.coas.oregonstate.edu*
Monthly average files are located in:
/pub/netCDF/<domain>/Monthly/<model>
Decadal average files are located in:
/pub/netCDF/<domain>/Decadal/<model>
As an example, to get files for PNW and the NCEP run the path would be:
/pub/netCDF/PNW/Monthly/NCEP.
We recommend using an ftp client rather than a browser to avoid problems that can occur with browsers.

High resolution images (600 dpi) in Portable Network Graphics (PNG) format are available for download at *http://pubs.usgs.gov/of/2011/1238/*.

netCDF File Overview and Naming Conventions

The naming convention for our simulations and their output is based on the driving GCM. The surface and near-surface variables are written into files that contain 1 year of monthly values. Metadata for the model configurations, mapping projections and included data are documented in the netCDF files. The attributes and structure of the files are mostly CF1.0 compliant; however, we diverge from compliance in some cases, particularly in the form of the netCDF files that are downloaded via the interactive Thredds downloading application.

The naming convention for standard monthly and daily average netCDF files is:

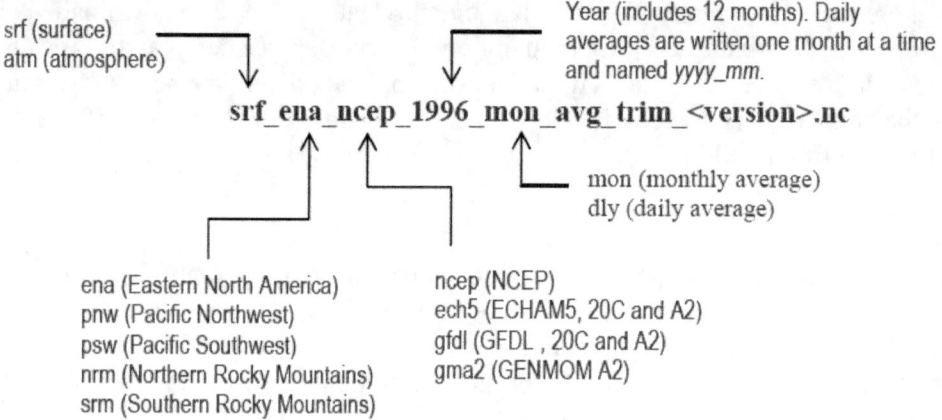

The naming convention for decadal averages is similar:

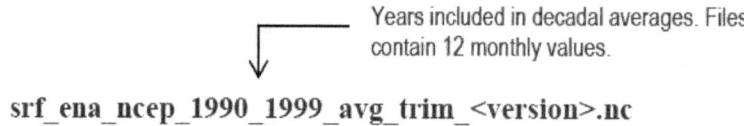

In the file names, "trim" indicates that the raw model output files have been processed to remove the sponge boundary region around the outside of the domain and "<version>" indicates the current version of the files, which is "v4" at the time this document was written.

Appendix B. Metadata.

Surface variables[1]

Average anemometer temperature (TA, ºC): 2-meter air temperature.

Average maximum anemometer temperature (TAMAX, ºC): 2-meter maximum air temperature.

Average minimum anemometer temperature (TAMIN, ºC): 2-meter minimum air temperature.

Absolute maximum anemometer temperature (TAMAXA, ºC): Value of the maximum 2-meter air temperature that occurred during the given time period.

Absolute minimum anemometer temperature (TAMINA, ºC): Value of the minimum 2-meter air temperature that occurred during the given time period.

Average ground temperature (TG, ºC): Temperature of the surface averaged over the given time period.

Average maximum ground temperature (TGMAX, ºC): Maximum temperature of the surface averaged over the given time period.

Average minimum ground temperature (TGMIN, ºC): Minimum temperature of the surface averaged over the given time period.

Average foliage temperature (TF, ºC): Temperature of the foliage averaged over the given time period.

Number of days with TA < 0ºC (T0, count): For daily averages: total number of 3-hr periods in which the absolute air temperature was below 0ºC. For monthly averages: total number of days in which the absolute air temperature was below 0ºC.

Number of days with TA > 33ºC (T33, count): For daily averages: total number of 3-hr periods in which the absolute air temperature was above 33ºC. For monthly averages: total number of days in which the absolute air temperature was above 33ºC.

---

[1] Averages, totals and counts are for model grid boxes. Latitude and longitudes are for the center of the grid box.

Growing degree days, base 10°C (GDD10, count): Growing degree days based on a 10°C threshold. Calculated as (McMaster and Wilhelm (1997), Agricultural and Forest Meteorology, 87(4):291-300, doi:10.1016/S0168-1923(97)00027-0):

$$GDD_{10} = \frac{TA_{max} - TA_{min}}{2.0} - 10 \quad ,$$

where TA_{max} is the daily maximum

$\qquad TA_{min}$ is the minimum daily temperature

growing degree days are accumulated only if the computed quantity is greater than zero.
Growing degree days base 5°C (GDD5, count): As above based on a threshold of 5°C.

Cooling degree days base 22°C (CDD, count): Cooling degree days (CDD) based on a 22°C threshold (T_{base}). CDDs are accumulated when the air temperature > 22°C and are calculated as:

$$DD = 0 \; if \; TA_{max} \leq T_{base}$$

$$DD = \frac{TA_{max} - T_{base}}{4.0} \; if \; \frac{TA_{max} + TA_{min}}{2.0} < T_{base}$$

$$DD = \frac{TA_{max} - T_{base}}{2.0} - \frac{T_{base} - TA_{min}}{4.0} \; if \; TA_{min} \leq T_{base}$$

$$DD = \frac{TA_{max} + TA_{min}}{2.0} - T_{base} \; if \; TA_{base} < T_{min}$$

Heating degree days base 15.5°C (HDD, count): Heating degree days (HDD) based on a 15.5°C threshold (T_{base}). HDDs are accumulated when the air temperature is < 15.5°C and are calculated as:

$$DD = 0 \; if \; TA_{base} \leq T_{min}$$

$$DD = \frac{TA_{base} - T_{min}}{4.0} \; if \; \frac{TA_{max} + TA_{min}}{2.0} > T_{base}$$

$$DD = \frac{TA_{base} - T_{min}}{2.0} - \frac{T_{max} - TA_{base}}{4.0} \; if \; TA_{max} \geq T_{base}$$

$$DD = T_{base} - \frac{TA_{max} + TA_{min}}{2.0} \; if \; TA_{max} < T_{base}$$

Solar radiation incident at the surface (SWI, W m^{-2}): Incoming solar radiation at the surface. The value is determined by insolation at the top and processes and properties of the atmosphere such as scattering and reflection by clouds and aerosols.

Net solar radiation absorbed (SWN, W m^{-2}): Incoming solar radiation absorbed at the surface. The value is determined by incident solar radiation and the albedo or reflectivity (α) of the surface: $\Phi_n = (1-\alpha)\Phi_i$ specified in the model. Albedo varies by date to account for surface changes and the angle of the sun.

Downward longwave radiation (LWD, W m^{-2}): Atmospheric longwave radiation flux at the surface.

Net longwave radiation (LWN, W m^{-2}): Net longwave radiation at the surface determined as the algebraic sum of incoming longwave (defined above) minus outgoing longwave, which is determined by the surface temperature and emissivity, and is radiated upward by the surface.

Sensible heat flux (SH, Wm^{-2}): Turbulent heat flux that occurs when the temperature of the surface differs from that of the overlying air. It is a function of temperature, atmospheric stability, wind speed and properties of the surface.

Evapotranspiration (ET, mm d^{-1}): Total evaporation from open water, land and vegetation. Can be converted to latent heat flux (the heat that is stored in water vapor) LE = λE where λ is the latent heat of vaporization.

Total precipitation (RT, mm d^{-1}): Total liquid water precipitation determined as the combined total of convective (associated, for example, with localized thunderstorms) and dynamic (associated with fronts).

Total convective precipitation in RT (RC, mm d^{-1}): The convective component of RT above.

Number of precipitation events P < 2 mm per 6h (3h) period (P2, count): Count of events having total precipitation less than 2 mm. The 6-hr (3-hr) period is the time step at which the data are written out by the model. This variable is part of a binning process that can be used to assess frequency of events in various categories.

Number of precipitation events 2 ≤ P < 10 mm per 6h (3h) period (P2_P10, count): Count of events having total precipitation greater than or equal to 2 mm and less than 10 mm. The 6-hr (3-hr) period is the time step at which the data are written out by the model. This variable is part of a binning process that can be used to assess frequency of events in various categories.

Number of precipitation events 10 ≤ P < 25 mm per 6h (3h) period (P10_P25, count): Count of events having total precipitation greater than or equal to 10 mm and less than 25 mm. The 6-hr (3-hr) period is the time step at which the data are written out by the model. This variable is part of a binning process that can be used to assess frequency of events in various categories.

Number of precipitation events 25 ≤ P < 50 mm per 6h (3h) period (P25_P50, count): Count of events having total precipitation greater than or equal to 25 mm and less than 50 mm. The 6-hr (3-hr) period is the time step at which the data are written out by the model. This variable is part of a binning process that can be used to assess frequency of events in various categories.

Number of precipitation events 50 ≤ P < 100 mm per 6h (3h) period (P50_P100, count): Count of events having total precipitation greater than or equal to 50 mm and less than 100 mm. The 6-hr (3-hr) period is the time step at which the data are written out by the model. This variable is part of a binning process that can be used to assess frequency of events in various categories.

Number of precipitation events P ≥ 100 mm per 6h (3h) period (P100, count): Count of events having total precipitation greater than 100 mm. The 6-hr (3-hr) period is the time step at which the data are written out by the model. This variable is part of a binning process that can be used to assess frequency of events in various categories.

Convection precipitation < 1 mm per 6h (3h) period (CA1, count): Count of convective events having total precipitation less than 1 mm. The 6-hr (3-hr) period is the time step at which the data are written out by the model. This variable is part of a binning process that can be used to assess dry versus wet convective storms.

Convection precipitation ≥ 1 mm per 6h (3h) period (CA2, count): Count of convective events having total precipitation greater than or equal to 1 mm. The 6-hr (3-hr) period is the time step at which the data are written out by the model. This variable is part of a binning process that can be used to assess dry versus wet convective storms.

Snow water equivalent (SNOW, mm): Total liquid water equivalent in snowpack.

Anemometer specific humidity (QA, kg kg^{-1}): Specific humidity at 2 m. Expressed as m_w/m_t where m_w is the mass of water vapor (kg) and m_t is the total mass of air (kg).

Anemometer relative humidity (RHA, fraction): Relative humidity at 2 m.

Surface runoff from soil model (RNFS, mm d^{-1}): Surface runoff computed by the soil model in BATS.

Base flow from soil model, (RB, mm d^{-1}): Net flow out of the lowest soil level (3 m thick) in BATS.

Top layer soil model moisture (RMT, mm): Liquid water content in the top soil layer (10 cm thick) in BATS.

Root layer soil model moisture (SMR, mm): Liquid water content in the root soil layer (vegetation dependent, 1.0, 1.5 or 2.0 m thick) in BATS.

Total runoff (pseudo hydrograph) (TOTRNF, m^3 s^{-1}): Total runoff rate from a model grid square computed as the sum of surface runoff and base flow.

Anemometer eastward wind (U, m s^{-1}): Eastward vector wind component at 2 meters.

Anemometer northward wind (V, m s^{-1}): Northward vector wind component at 2 meters.

Number of 3-hr wind velocity events > 6 ms^{-1} (UMAG6, count): Count of the number of wind events that exceed 6 ms^{-1} at a 3-hr interval. This derived variable is used to assess dune mobility.

Maximum 10 m wind speed (W10MX, m s^{-1}): Maximum simulated wind speed at 10 m over the averaging period.

Planetary boundary layer height (ZPBL, m): The height or thickness of the planetary boundary layer, the lowest level of the atmosphere that interacts with and is influenced by the land/ocean surface.

Surface drag stress (DRAG, N m^{-2}): The shear stress over the land/ocean surface associated with wind. It is determined by properties of the surface (e.g., roughness, displacement height).

Surface pressure (PSRF, hPa): Atmospheric pressure on the model surface. Surface pressure varies with elevation of the model surface.

Minimum surface pressure (PSMIN, hPa): Minimum surface pressure over the averaging period.

Sea level pressure: Atmospheric pressure at sea level. SLP is a primary control of surface wind patterns.

Total cloud fraction (TOTCLD, fraction): Total cloud cover in the model. The RegCM uses random overlap to determine cloud cover from types present in the vertical levels. Total cloud cover C_T is determined

as: $C_T = 1 - \prod_{l=1}^{nlevels} \left(1 - f_l\right)$, where f_l is the cloud fraction of model level l and $nlevels$ is the number of vertical levels

(23). See Weare, BC, (2001) *Climate Dynamics* 17:143-150.

3-Dimensional Variables on Atmospheric Pressure Levels

Cloud water mixing ratio (QC_p, kg kg^{-1}): Water mixing ratio in clouds. Determined by m_w / m_d where m_w is the mass of water vapor (kg) and m_d is the mass of dry air (kg).

Atmospheric mixing ratio (QD_p, kg kg^{-1}): As above, but for the total atmosphere.

Relative humidity (RH_p, fraction): As defined above.

Dew point temperature (TD_p, ºC): The temperature to which moist air (as determined by air temperature and mixing ratio) must be cooled to change the phase of water vapor to liquid water.

Horizontal divergence (DIV_p, m s^{-1}): An area in the atmosphere where air mass is decreasing through time. Determined by wind flow and associated with cyclonic development and activity in the atmosphere: upper level divergence is accompanied by lower level convergence and upward motion leading to potential precipitation events. For more information see:
http://amsglossary.allenpress.com/glossary/search?p=1&query=horizontal+divergence&submit=Search

Geopotential height (HGT_p, m): The height of constant pressure levels in the atmosphere. Commonly levels at 950, 850, 700, 500 and 300 hPa are used to diagnose and predict atmospheric circulation patterns at regional and hemispheric scales.

Potential temperature (TH_p, ºC): The temperature that an unsaturated parcel of dry air at a given pressure would attain if the parcel was brought adiabatically to a standard pressure (typically 1000 hPa). Potential temperature is associated with vertical static stability and thus convection in the atmosphere. For more information see: *http://amsglossary.allenpress.com/glossary/search?p=1&query=potential+temperature&submit=Search*

Atmospheric temperature (T_p, ºC): Temperature on model pressure levels.

Eastward wind (U_p, m s⁻¹): Eastward wind vector on model pressure levels.

Northward wind (V_p, m s⁻¹): Northward wind vector on model pressure levels.

Horizontal vorticity (VOR_p, m s⁻¹): Rotation of air masses around a vertical axis. In the Northern Hemisphere, clockwise rotation (positive vorticity) associated with anticyclonic flow and counter clockwise (negative vorticity) with cyclonic flow. Associated with vertical motions and development of convective activity. For more information see: *http://amsglossary.allenpress.com/glossary/search?id=potential-vorticity1*

Moist static energy (MSE_p, m² s⁻²): A measure of the total potential and kinetic energy and latent heat derived from water vapor content of an air parcel. Also associated with convective development. http://amsglossary.allenpress.com/glossary/search?p=1&query=moist+static&submit=Search

Omega (OMEGA_p, Pa s⁻¹): Vertical rising rate of air parcels. Associated with vorticty. Provides a measure of large scale rising and sinking motions in the atmosphere. Negative values indicate rising and a tendency for convection and positive values indicate sinking motions associated with adiabatic warming and high pressure. For more information see: *http://amsglossary.allenpress.com/glossary/search?p=1&query=omega+equation&submit=Search*

Terrain ht, Vegetation codes, Axes and Projection Information

Terrain ht (ht, m): Elevation of model grid squares.

Pressure-coordinate: Pressure levels (hPa) in the processed output: 100., 200, 300, 400, 500, 600, 700, 750, 800, 850, 900, 950, 1000.

Time-coordinate: Time step of data. The axis has an unlimited dimension and the units are in the standard format of days since 1900-01-01.

BATS surface type codes: See below.

x-coordinate: Horizontal distance coordinates of the grid centers.

y-coordinate: Vertical distance coordinates of the grid centers.

Latitude: Latitude of the grid centers.

Longitude: Longitude of the grid centers.

Lambert_Conformal: Projection type used in the model.

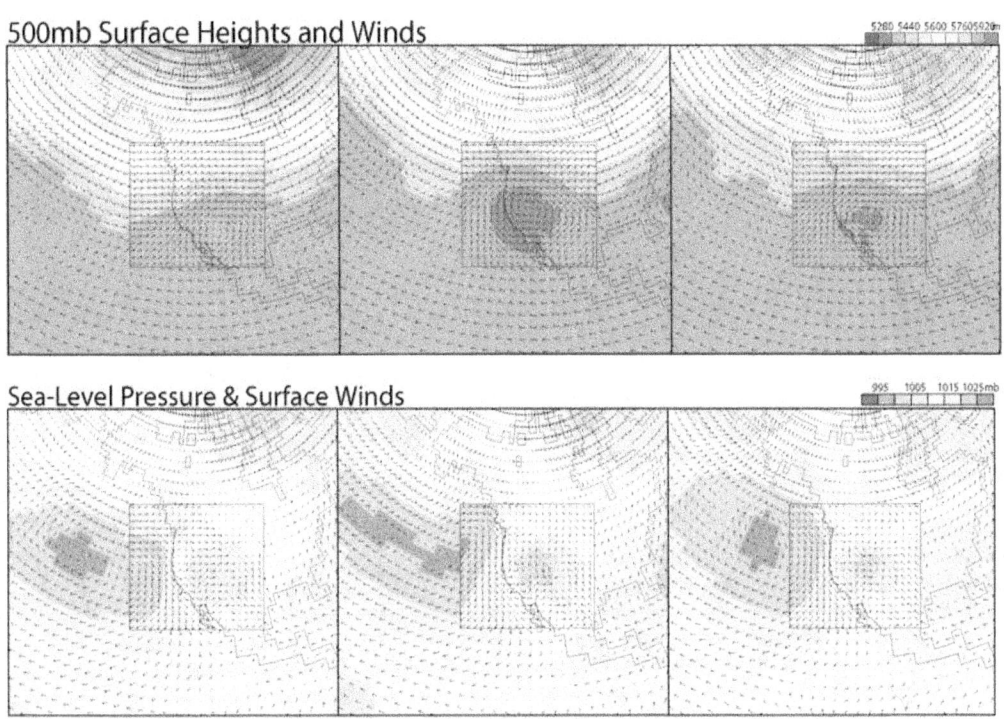

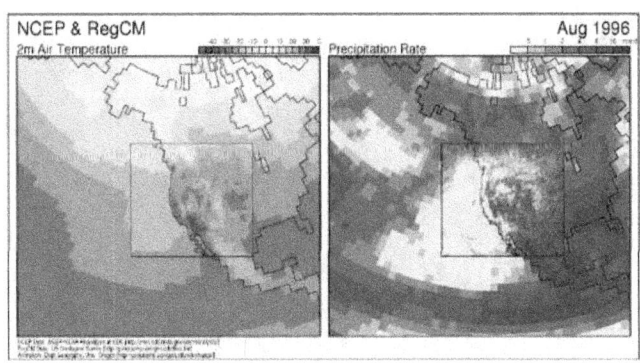

Figure 1. Nesting of the RegCM3 within a GCM (NOAA, NCEP). Large scale fields from global climate simulations are introduced to the regional model along the boundary indicated by the box. In this example, the grid spacing of the NCEP GCM is 2.5° latitude and longitude and the grid spacing of the RegCM3 is 45 km. Top row) weekly average 500-mb heights and wind vectors for August 1996, middle row) weekly average sea surface pressure and surface wind vectors for August 1996, and bottom row) mean temperature and precipitation rate for August 1996. Figures from Hostetler and others (2003).

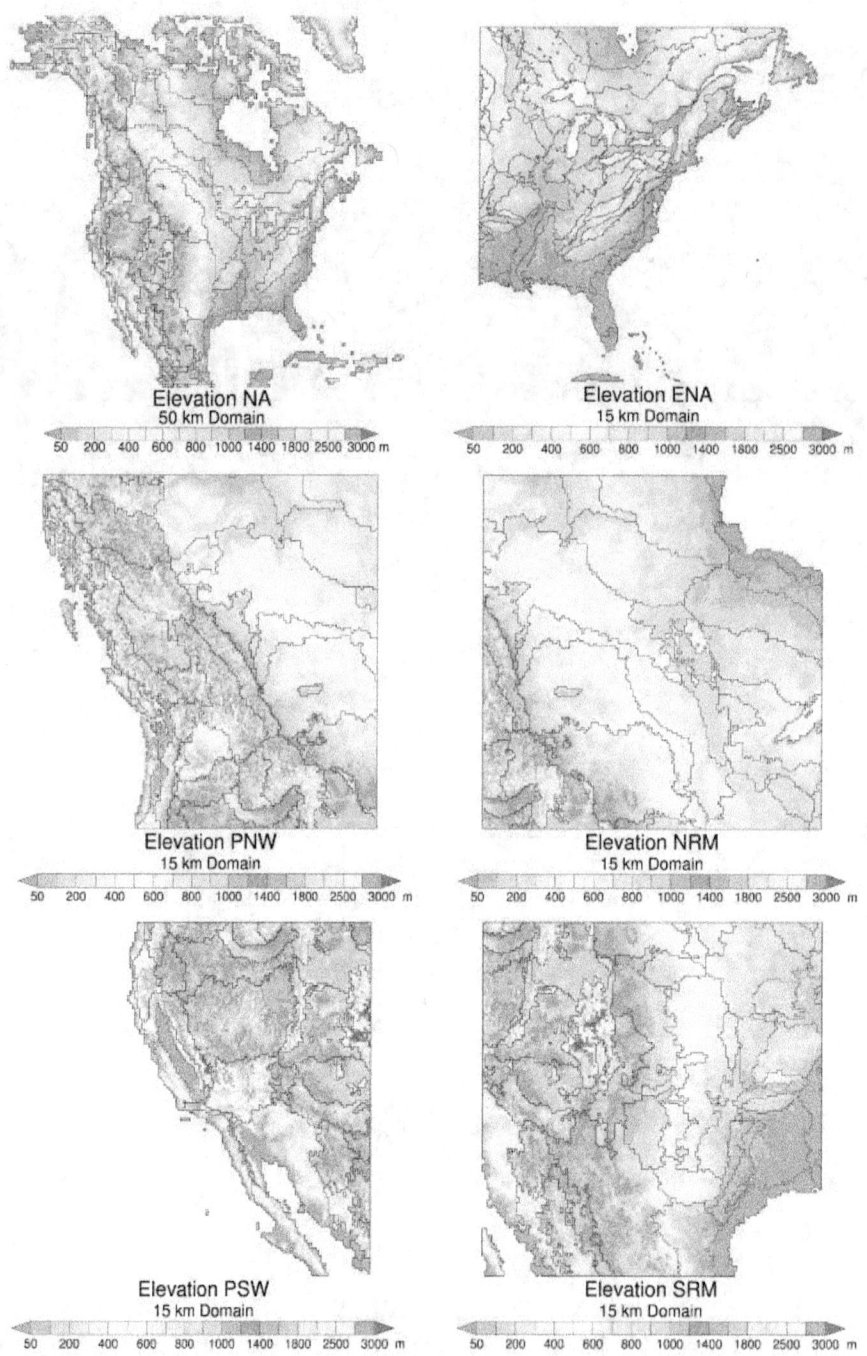

Figure 2. Topography and extent of the six RegCM3 domains. A 50-km grid spacing is used for the North American domain and a 15-km grid spacing is used for Eastern (ENA) and Western North America (WNA). WNA is divided into four subregions: the Pacific Northwest (PNW), the Pacific Southwest (PSW), the Northern Rocky Mountains (NRM), and Southern Rocky Mountains (SRM). The subdivisions on the maps are the EPA Level II ecoregions (50-km domain) and the EPA Level III ecoregions (15-km domains).

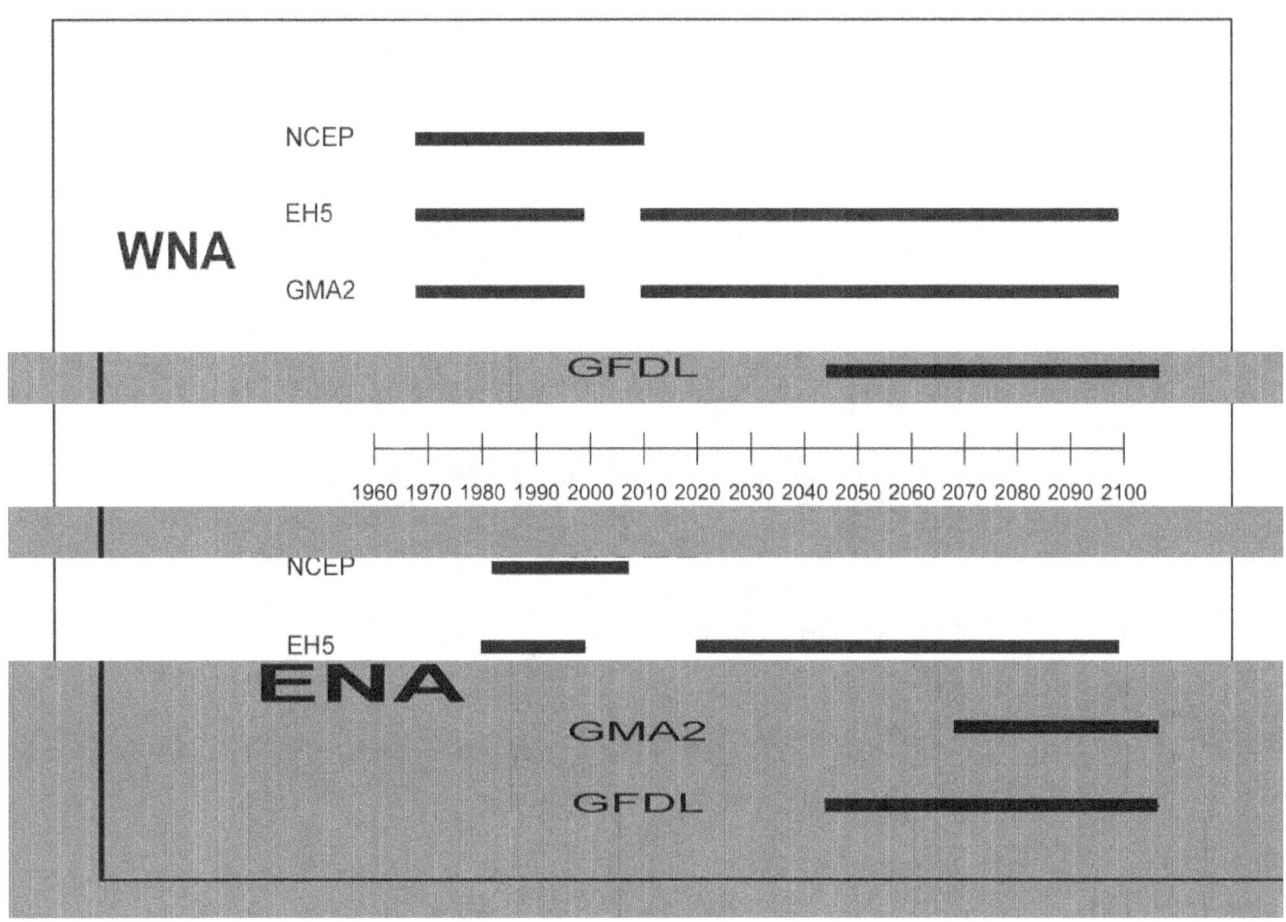

Figure 3. Time periods covered by the 15-km RegCM simulations for Western North America (WNA, top) and Eastern North America (ENA, bottom).

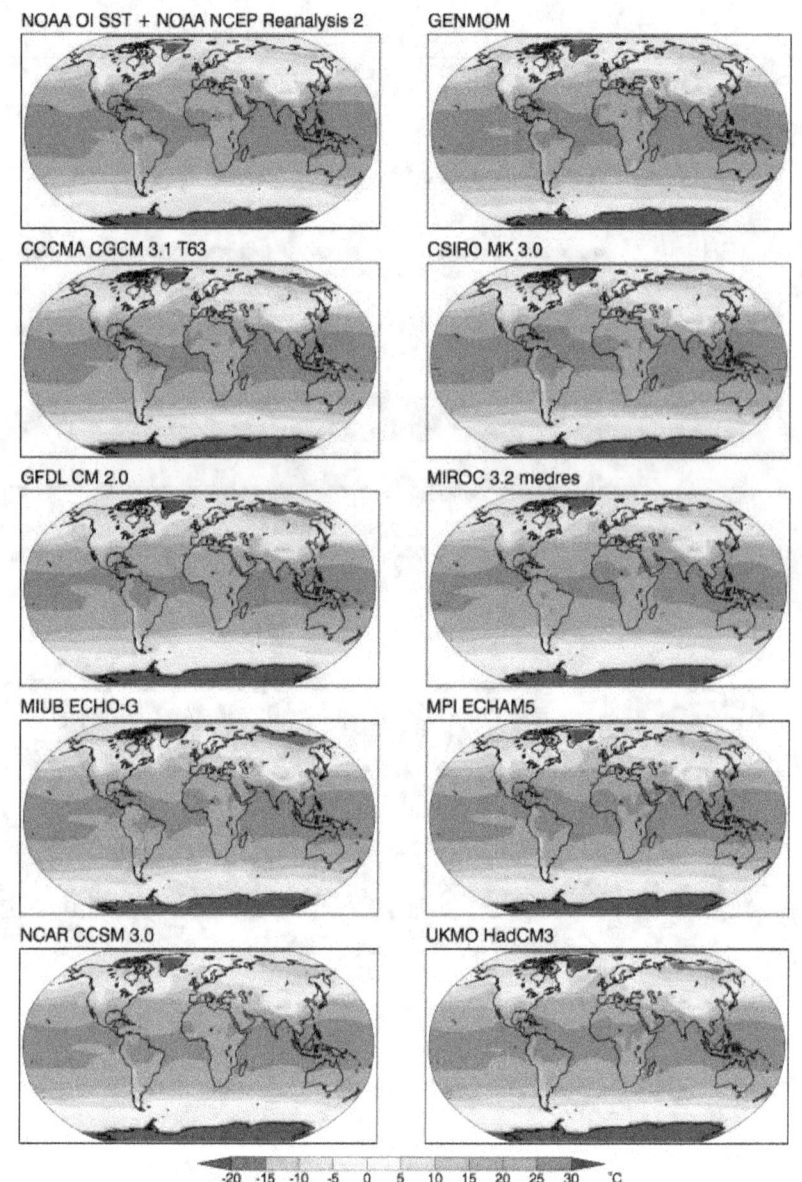

Figure 4. Mean annual 2-m air temperature climatologies simulated by GENMOM and a selected subgroup of eight global climate models used in the IPCC AR4 compared with the NOAA NCEP Reanalysis II (upper left) climatology. GENMOM, GFDL CM2.0, and ECHAM5 were used in our regional model simulations. The model names correspond to the respective modeling centers and numbers refer to model version. Full descriptions and details are provided on the web sites of the modeling centers. CCCMA: Canadian Centre for Climate Modelling and Analysis, Canada, CSIRO MK: Commonwealth Scientific and Industrial Research Organisation (CSIRO) Atmospheric Research, Australia, GFDL: U.S. Department of Commerce/National Oceanic and Atmospheric Administration (NOAA)/Geophysical Fluid Dynamics Laboratory (GFDL), USA, MIROC: Center for Climate System Research (University of Tokyo), National Institute for Environmental Studies, and Frontier Research Center for Global Change (JAMSTEC), Japan, MIUB ECHO-G: Meteorological Institute of the University of Bonn, Meteorological Research Institute of the Korea Meteorological Administration (KMA), and Model and Data Group, Germany/Korea, MPI ECHAM5: Max Planck Institute for Meteorology, Germany, NCAR CCSM: National Center for Atmospheric Research, USA, UKMO HadCM3: Hadley Centre for Climate Prediction and Research/Met Office, UK.

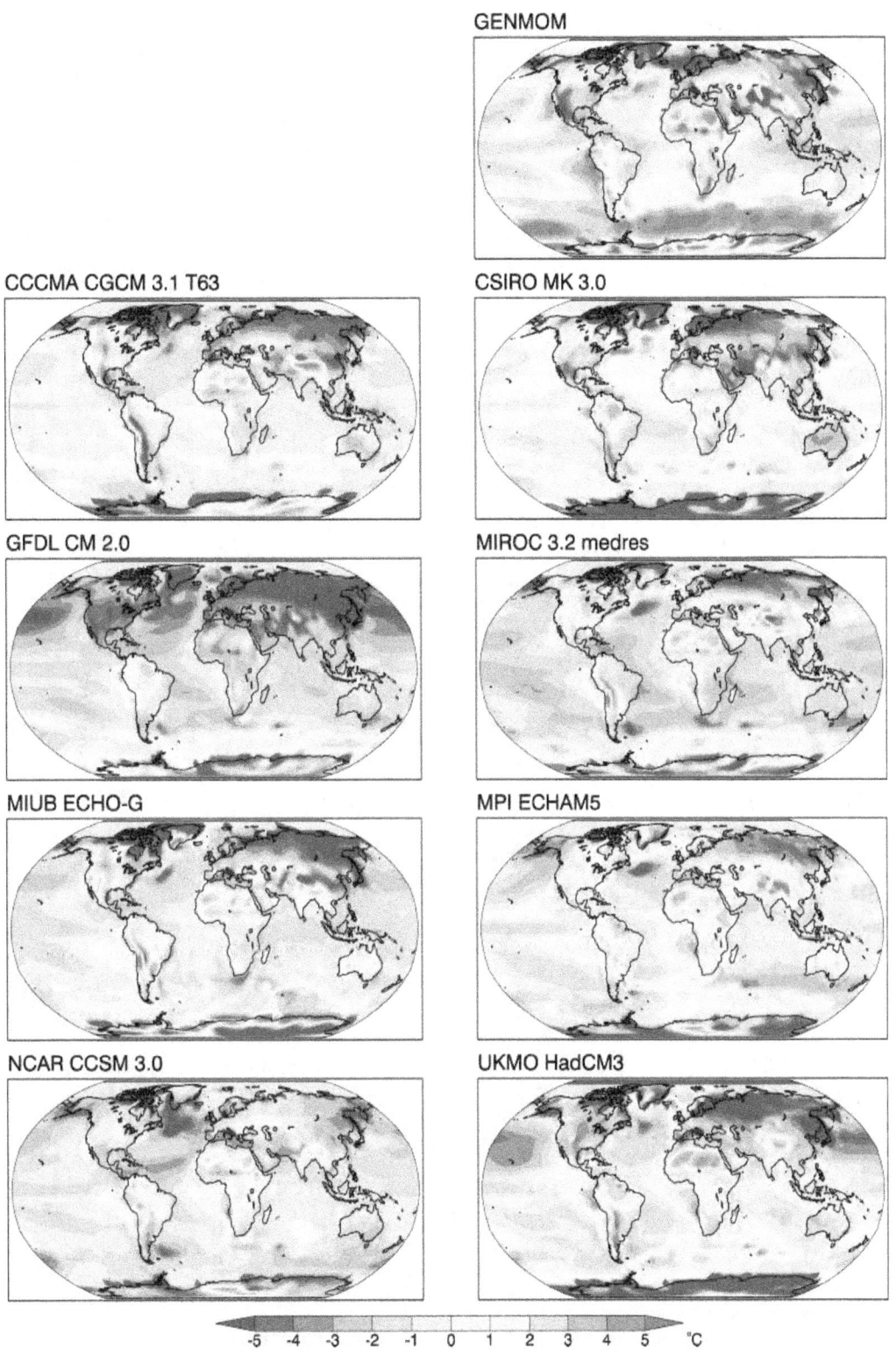

Figure 5. Differences (anomalies) between the simulated mean annual 2-m temperature climatologies and the NOAA NCEP Reanalysis II for GENMOM and a selected subgroup of eight global climate models used in the IPCC AR4. Model names are given in figure 4.

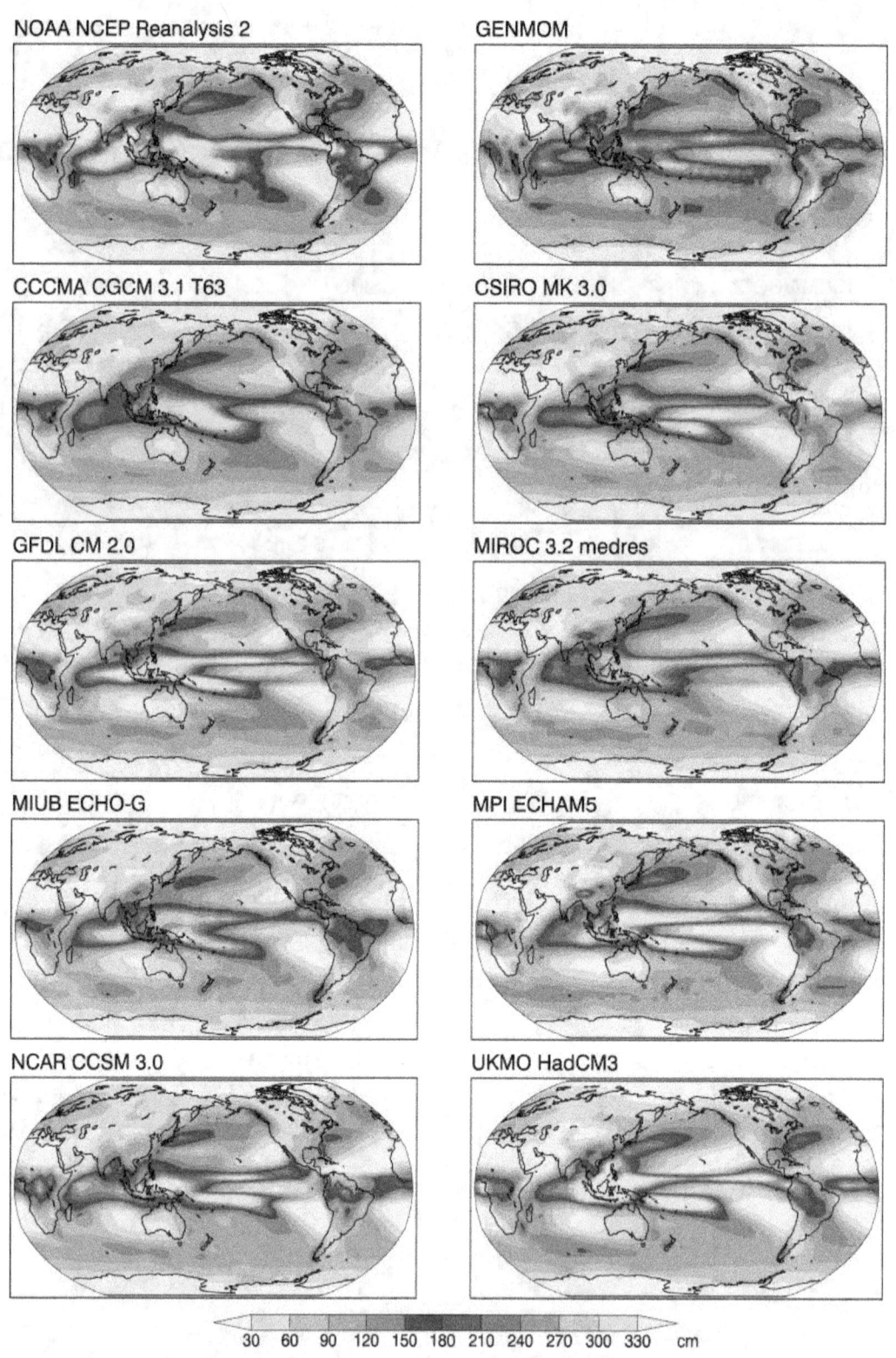

Figure 6. Mean annual precipitation climatologies simulated by GENMOM and a selected subgroup of eight global climate models used in the IPCC AR4 compared with the NOAA NCEP Reanalysis II (upper left) climatology. Model names are given in figure 4.

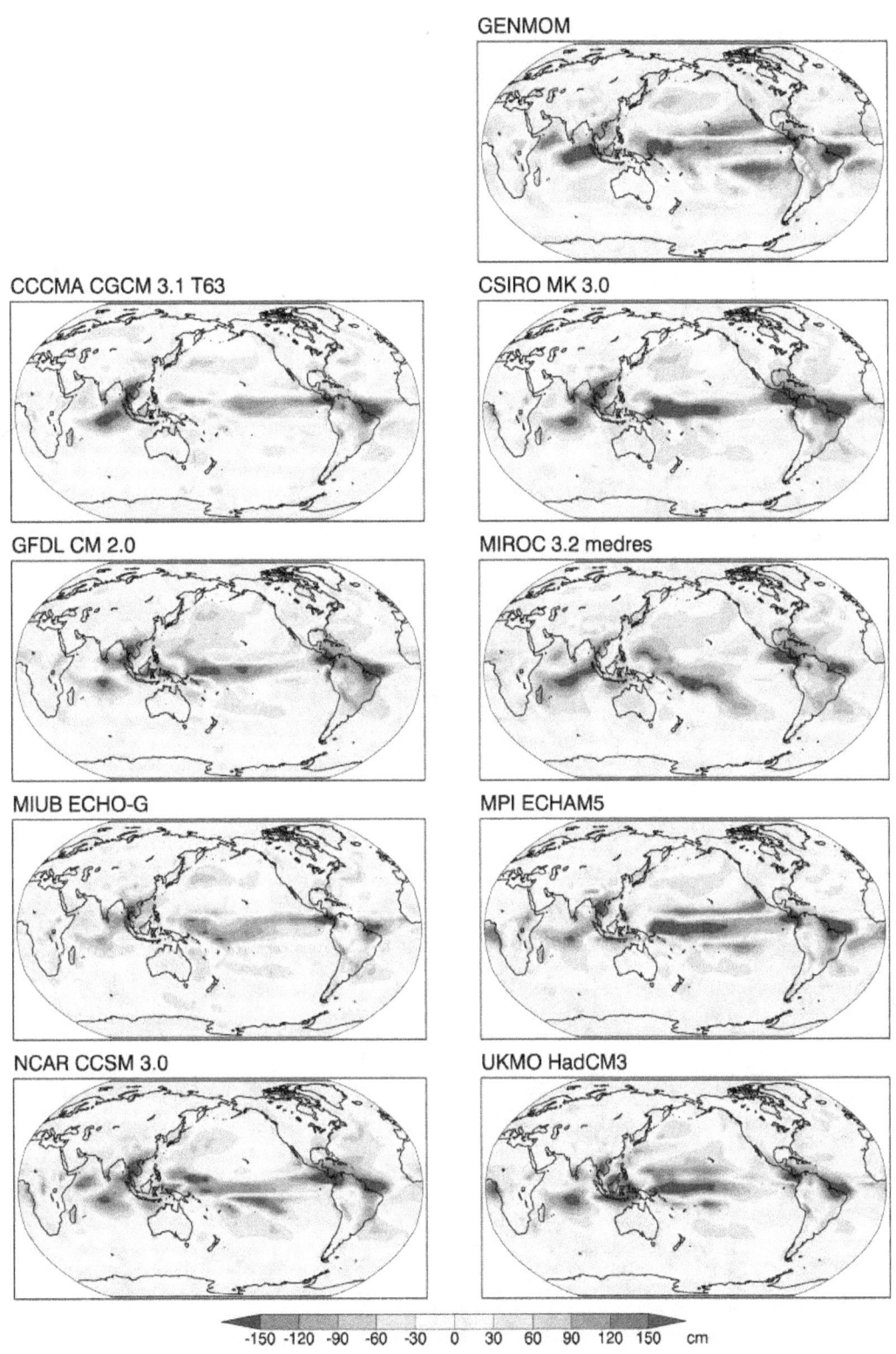

Figure 7. Differences (anomalies) between the simulated mean annual precipitation climatologies and the NOAA NCEP Reanalysis II for GENMOM and a selected subgroup of eight global climate models used in the IPCC AR4. Model names are given in figure 4.

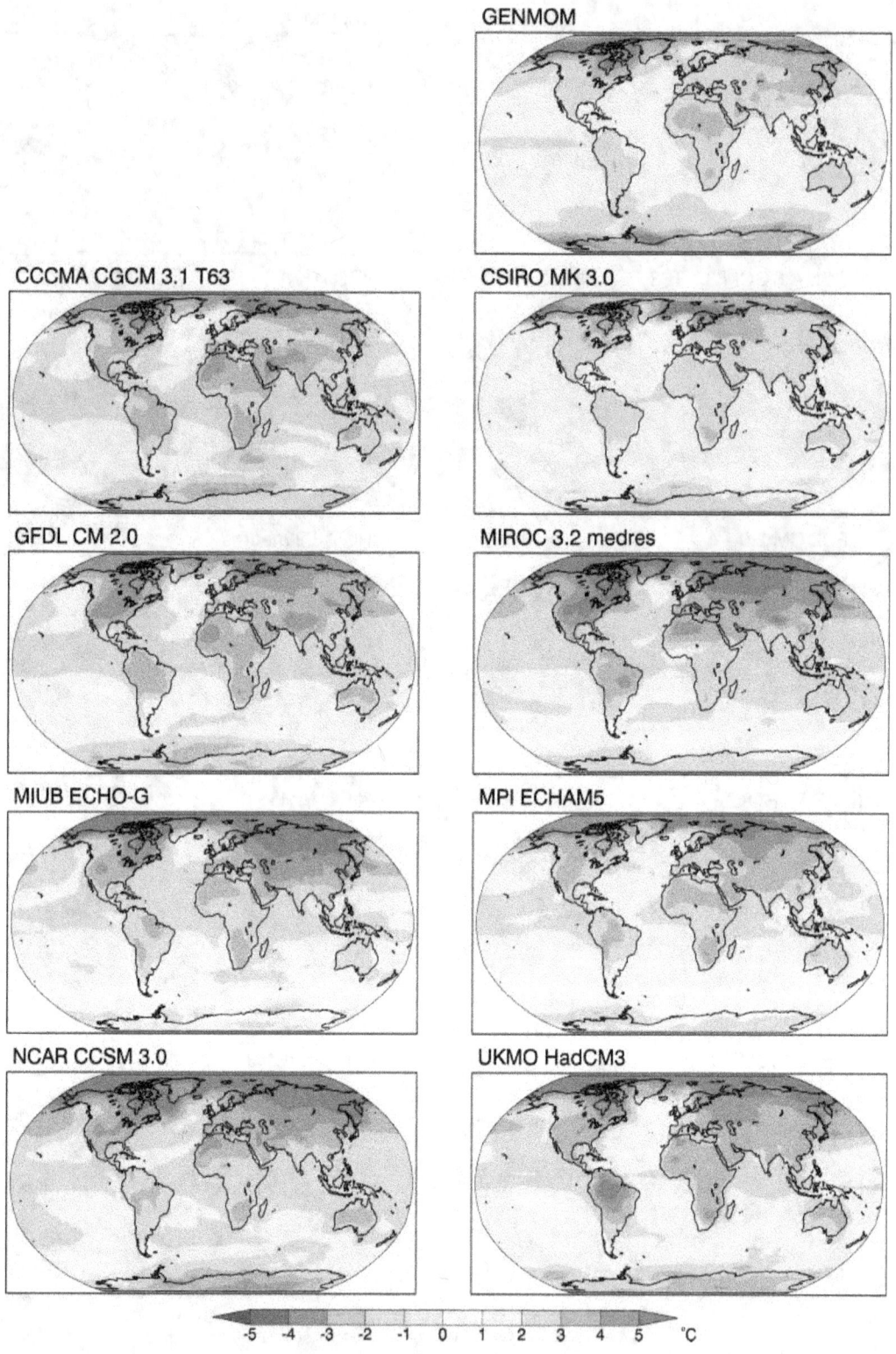

Figure 8. Mean annual 2-m temperature sensitivity to a doubling of atmospheric CO_2 concentration in GENMOM and a selected subgroup of eight global climate models used in the IPCC AR4. Model names are given in figure 4.

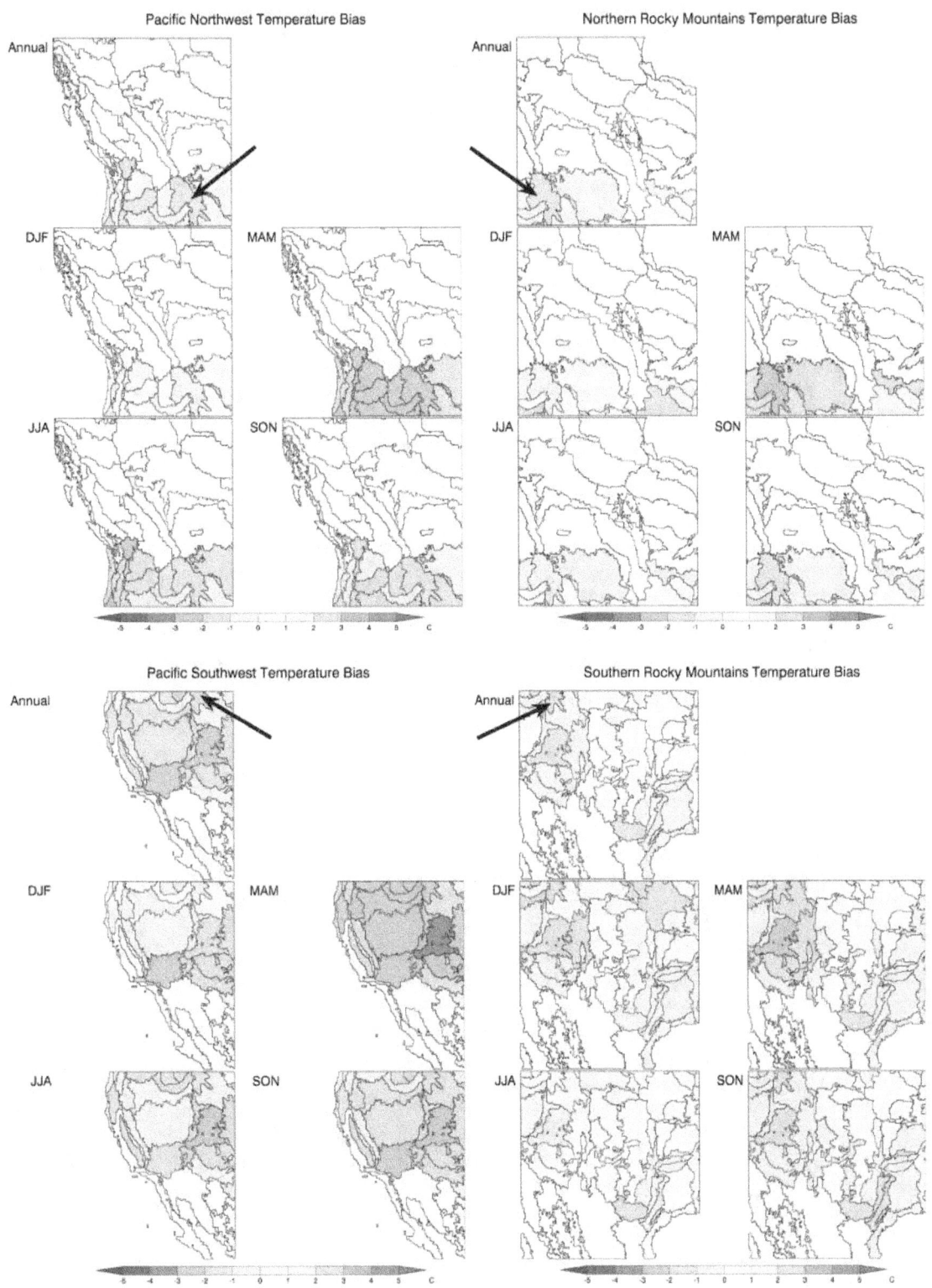

Figure 9. Annual and seasonal differences (biases) between simulated 2-m air temperatures and PRISM values averaged over the EPA Level III ecoregions for the WNA domains. The averaging period is 1985–1999. Clockwise from the upper left: Pacific Northwest, Northern Rocky Mountains, Southern Rocky Mountains, Pacific Southwest. The arrows point to the Middle Rockies ecoregion and are discussed in the text. PRISM data from Daly and others (1994).

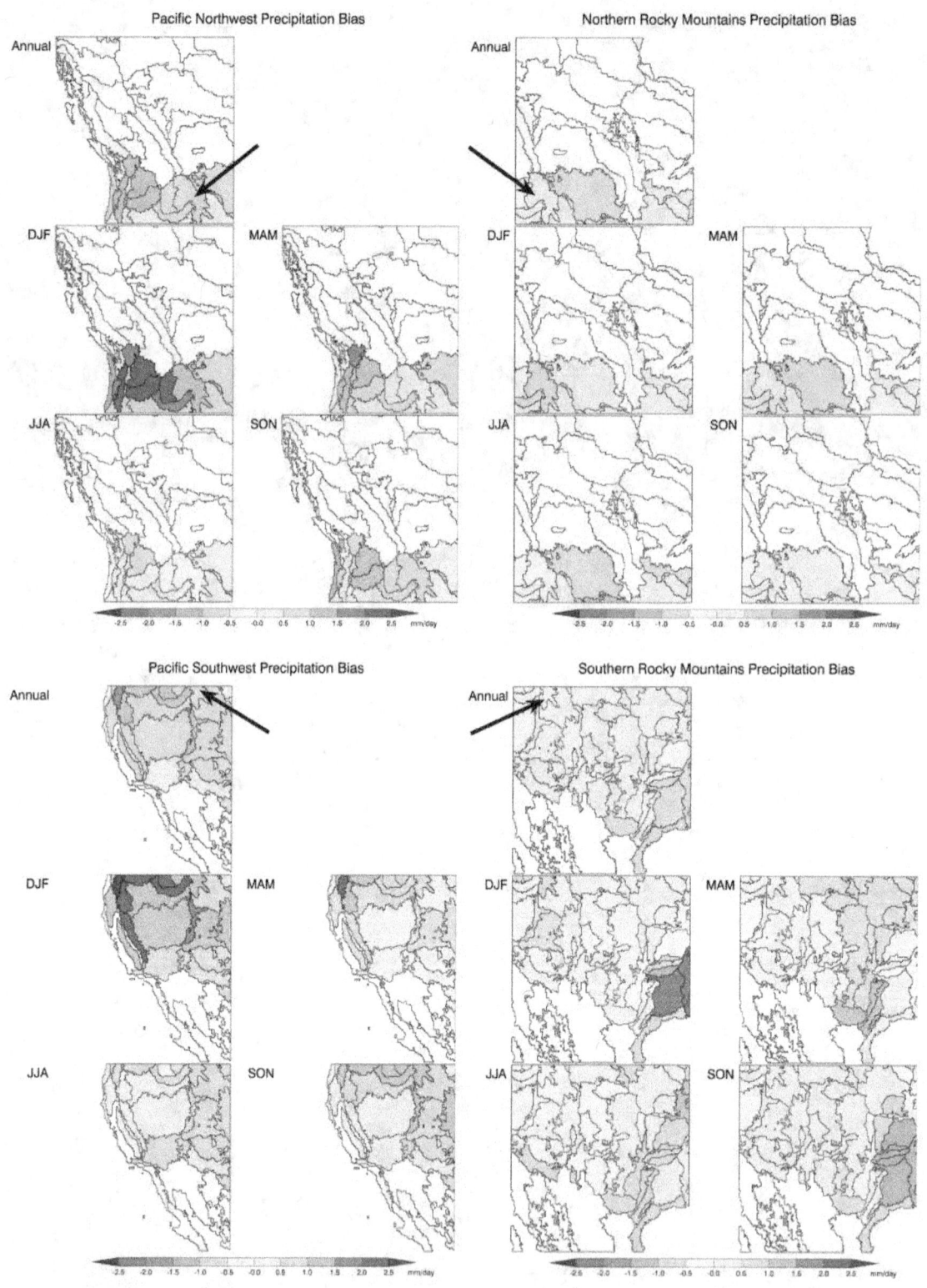

Figure 10. Annual and seasonal differences (biases) between simulated precipitation rates and PRISM values averaged over the EPA Level III ecoregions for the WNA domains. The averaging period is 1985–1999. Clockwise from the upper left: Pacific Northwest, Northern Rocky Mountains, Southern Rocky Mountains, Pacific Southwest. The arrows point to the Middle Rockies ecoregion and are discussed in the text. PRISM data from Daly and others (1994).

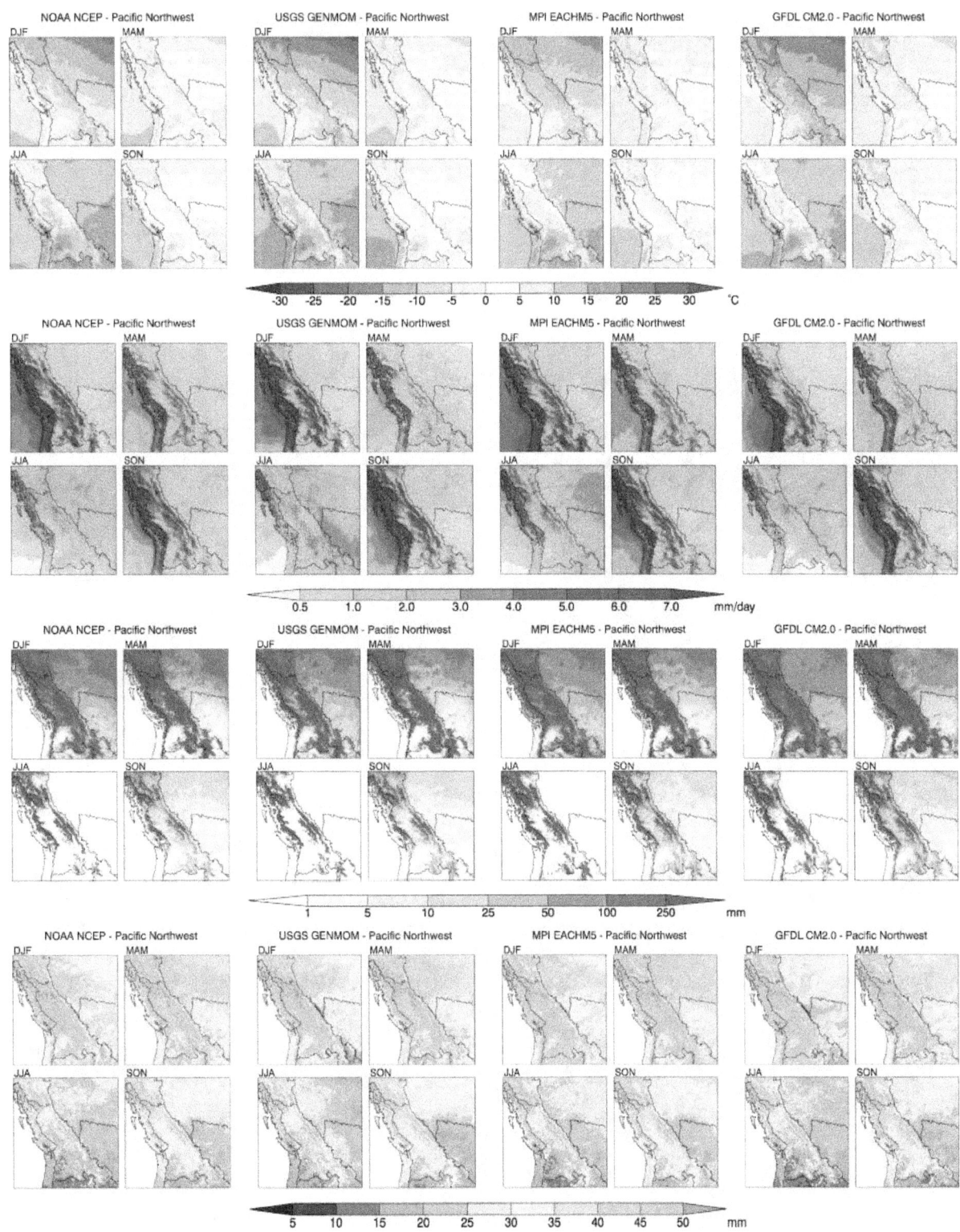

Figure 11. Seasonal average climatologies (averaging period is 1985-1999) over the PNW domain for the four RegCM3 simulations. Row 1: 2 m air temperature, row 2: precipitation rate, row 3: snow-water equivalent, and row 4: root-zone soil moisture.

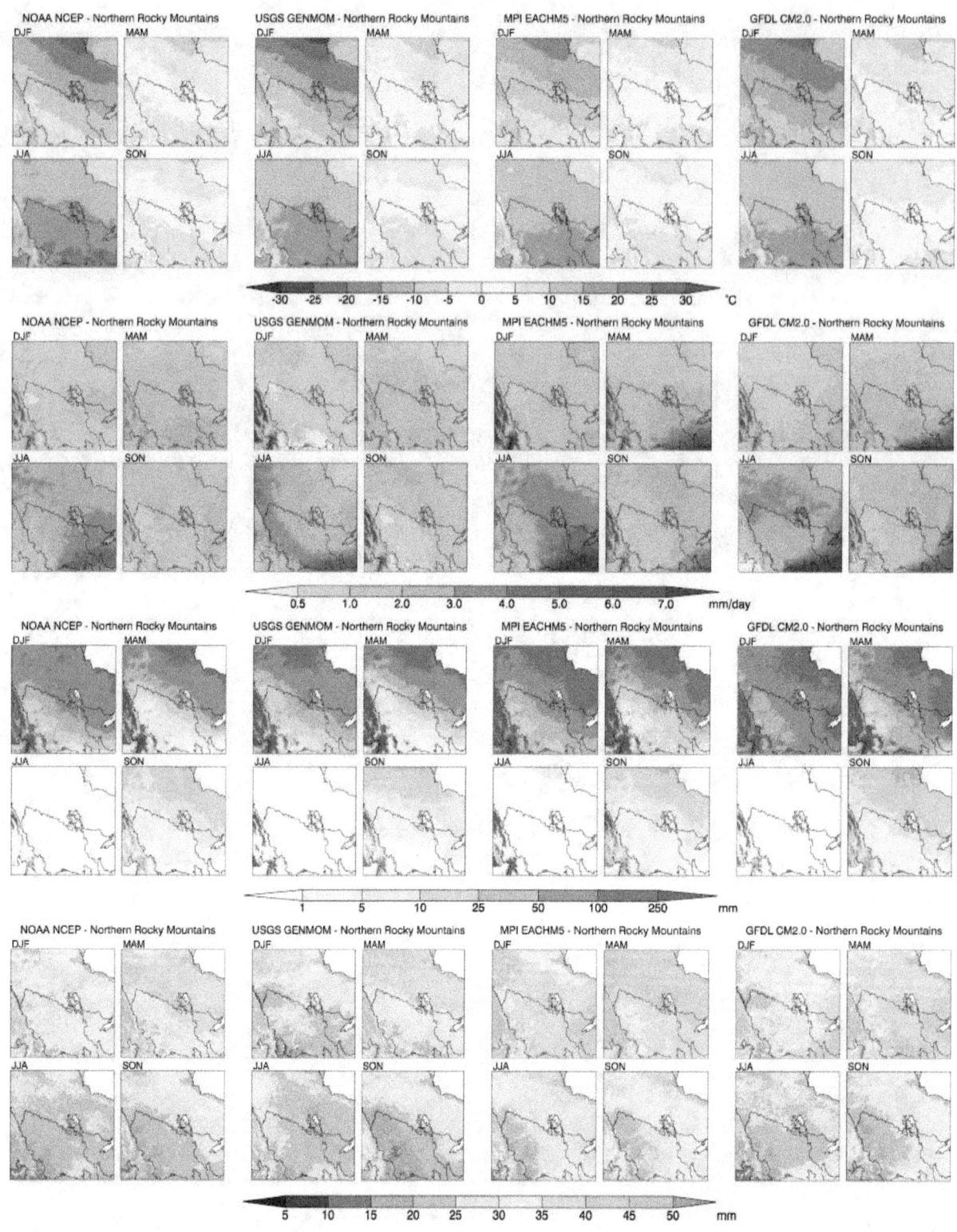

Figure 12. Seasonal average climatologies (averaging period is 1985–1999) over the NRM domain for the four RegCM3 simulations. Row 1: 2 m air temperature, row 2: precipitation rate, row 3: snow-water equivalent, and row 4: root-zone soil moisture.

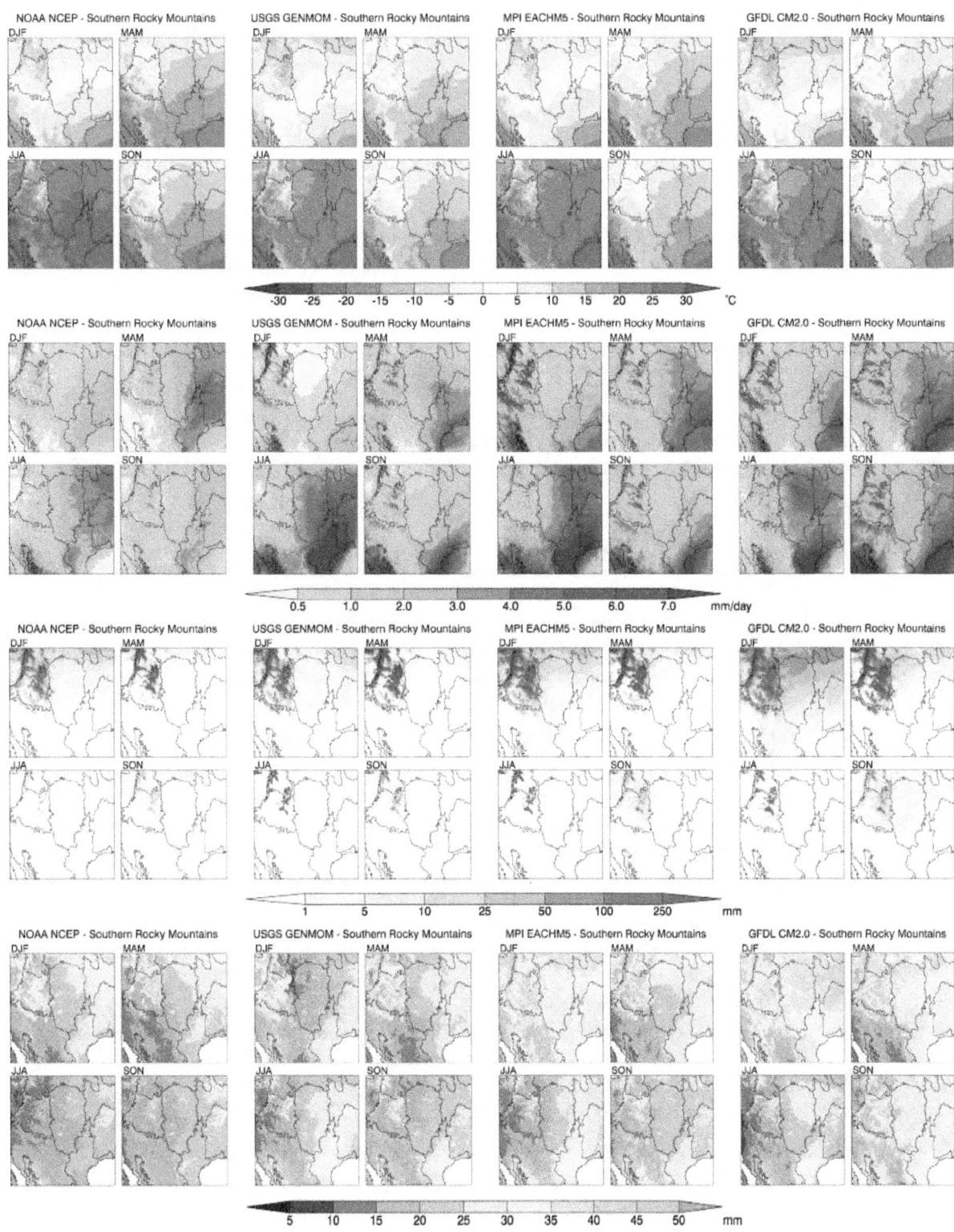

Figure 13. Seasonal average climatologies (averaging period is 1985–1999) over the SRM domain for the four RegCM3 simulations. Row 1: 2 m air temperature, row 2: precipitation rate, row 3: snow-water equivalent, and row 4: root-zone soil moisture.

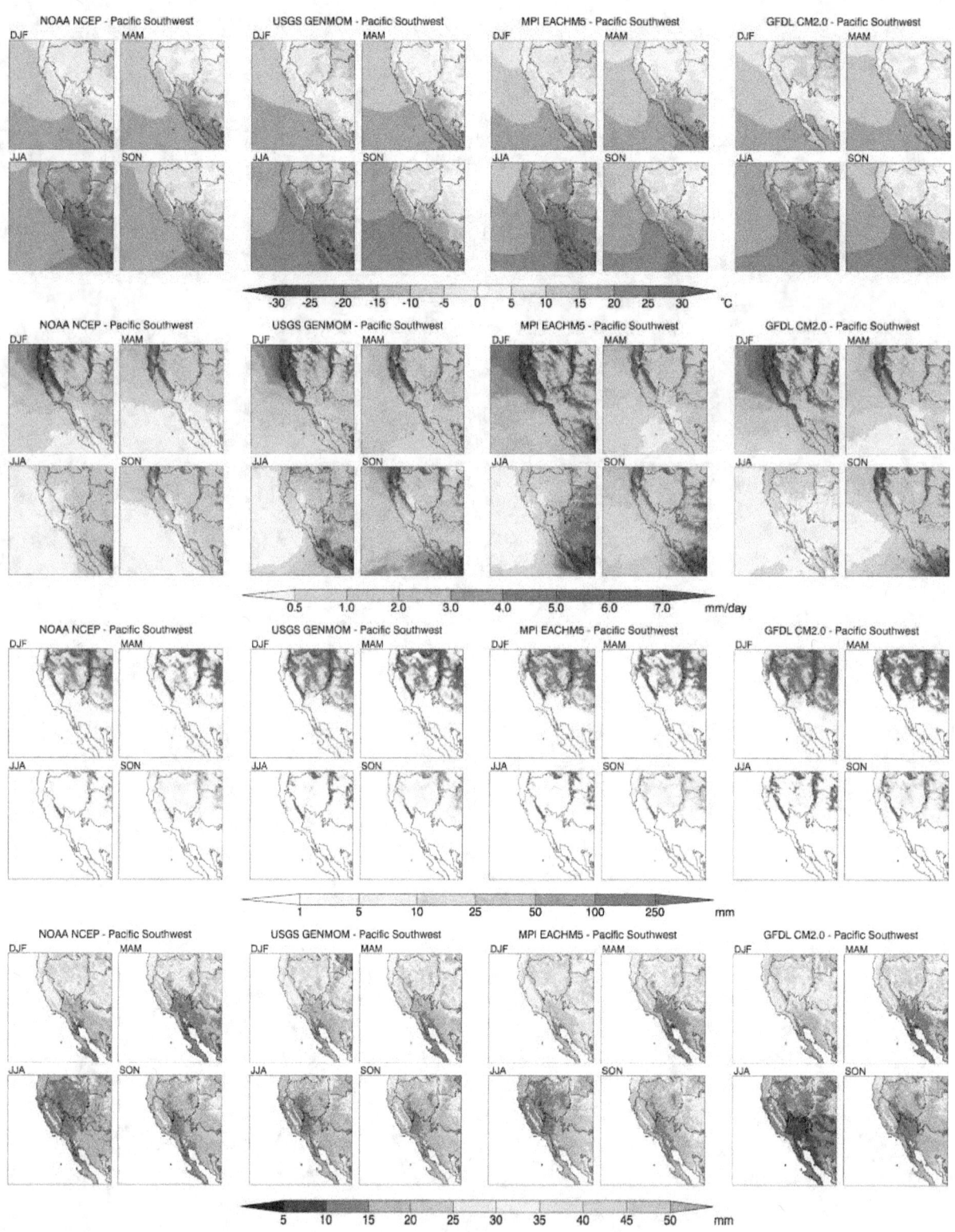

Figure 14. Seasonal average climatologies (averaging period is 1985–1999) over the PSW domain for the four RegCM3 simulations. Row 1: 2 m air temperature, row 2: precipitation rate, row 3: snow-water equivalent, and row 4: root-zone soil moisture.

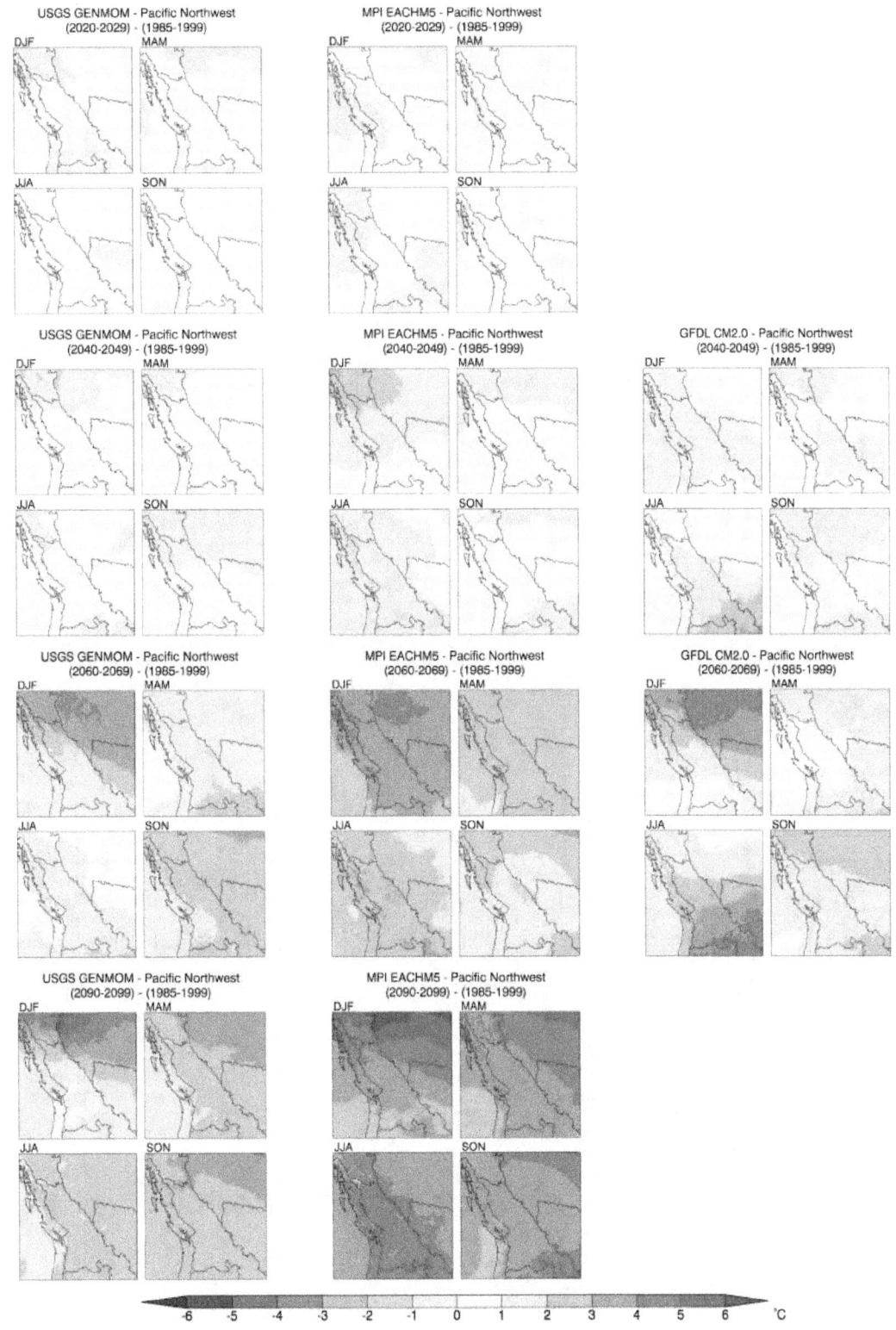

Figure 15. Differences between seasonal average 2-m air temperature climatologies for future decades (2020–2029, 2040–2049, 2060–2069, and 2090–2099) versus 1985–1999 over the PNW domain for the three RegCM3 ss. Column 1: GMA2, column 2: ECH5 and column 3: GFDL. Row 1: 2020–2029, row 2: 2040–2049, row 3: 2060–2069 and row 4: 2090–2099.

37

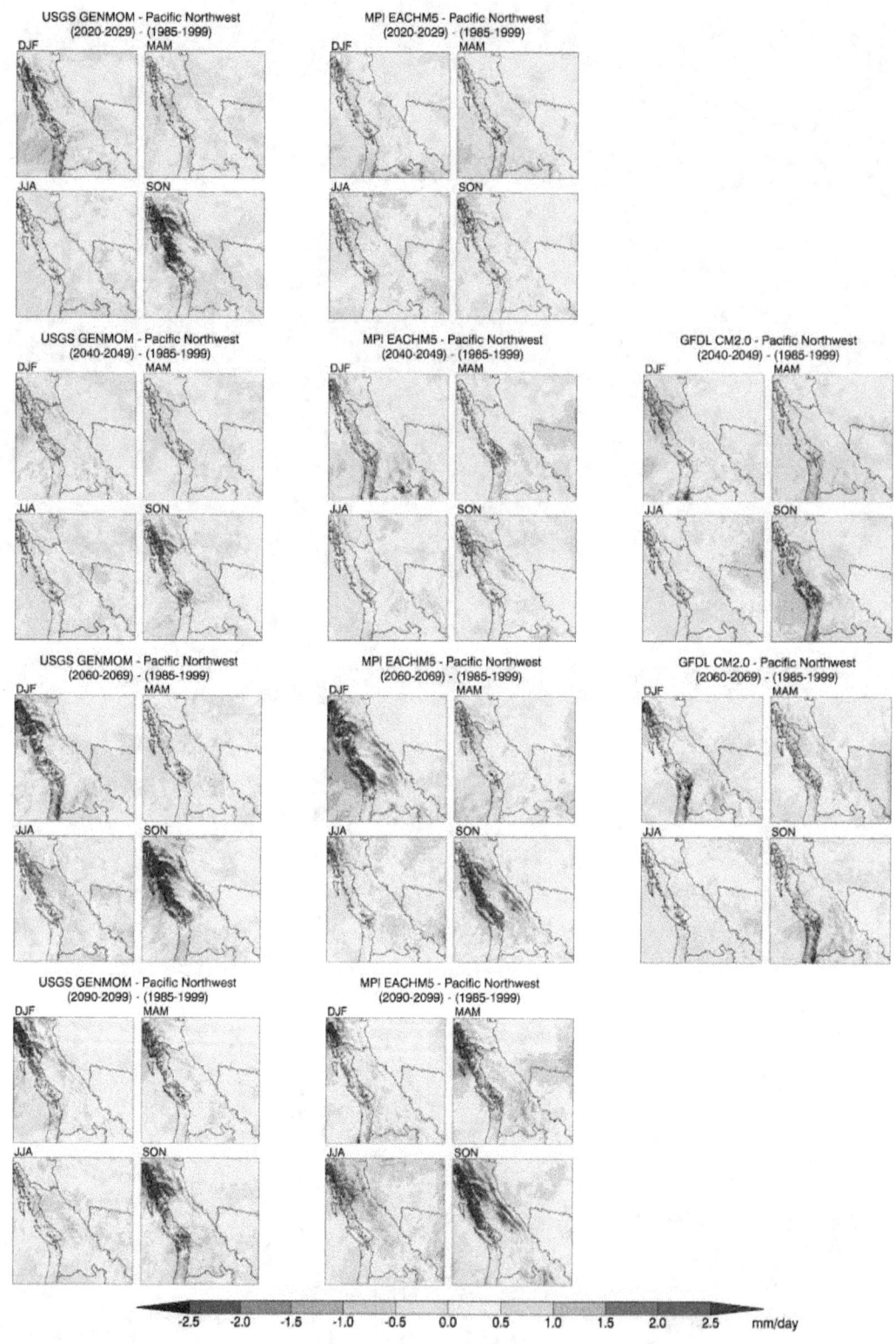

Figure 16. Differences between seasonal average precipitation climatologies for future decades (2020–2029, 2040–2049, 2060–2069, and 2090–2099) versus 1985–1999 over the PNW domain for the three RegCM3 projections. Column 1: GMA2, column 2: ECH5, and column 3: GFDL. Row 1: 2020–2029, row 2: 2040–2049, row 3: 2060–2069, and row 4: 2090–2099.

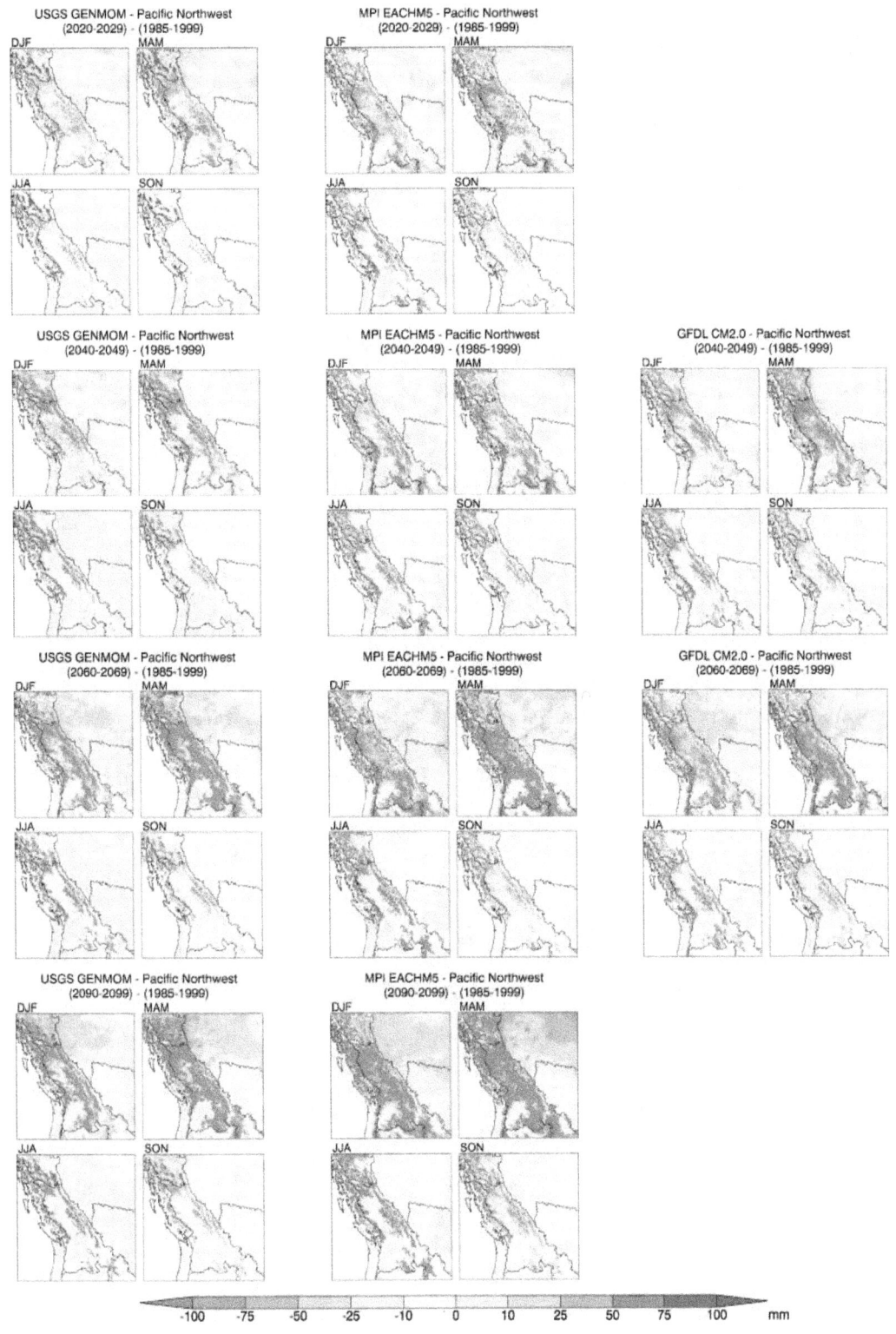

Figure 17. Differences between seasonal average snow water equivalent climatologies for future decades (2020–2029, 2040–2049, 2060–2069, and 2090–2099) versus 1985–1999 over the PNW domain for the three RegCM3 projections. Column 1: GMA2, column 2: ECH5, and column 3: GFDL. Row 1: 2020–2029, row 2: 2040–2049, row 3: 2060–2069, and row 4: 2090–2099.

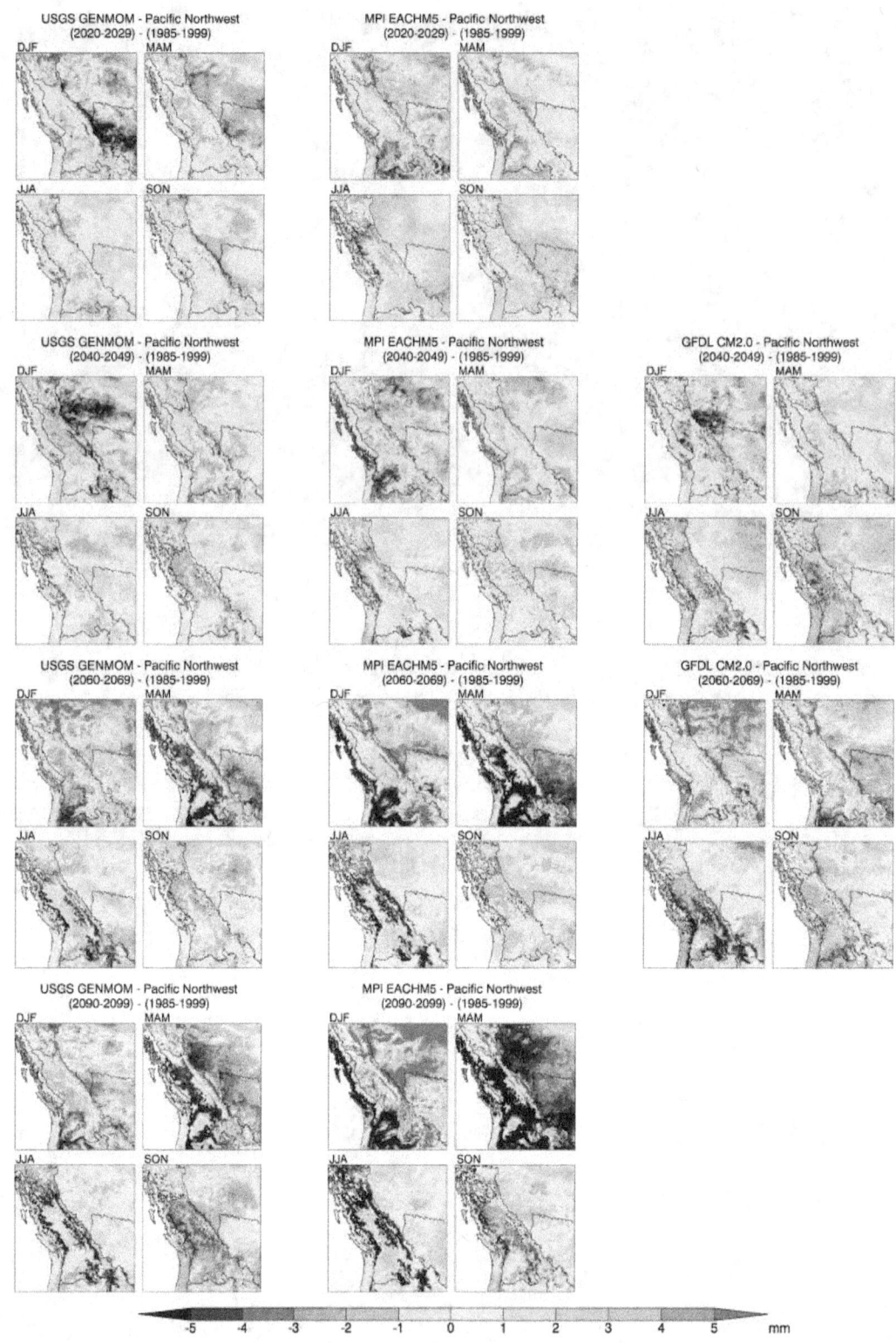

Figure 18. Differences between seasonal average root-zone soil moisture climatologies for future decades (2020–2029, 2040–2049, 2060–2069, and 2090–2099) versus 1985–1999 over the PNW domain for the three RegCM3 projections. Column 1: GMA2, column 2: ECH5 and column 3: GFDL. Row 1: 2020–2029, row 2: 2040–2049, row 3: 2060–2069, and row 4: 2090–2099.

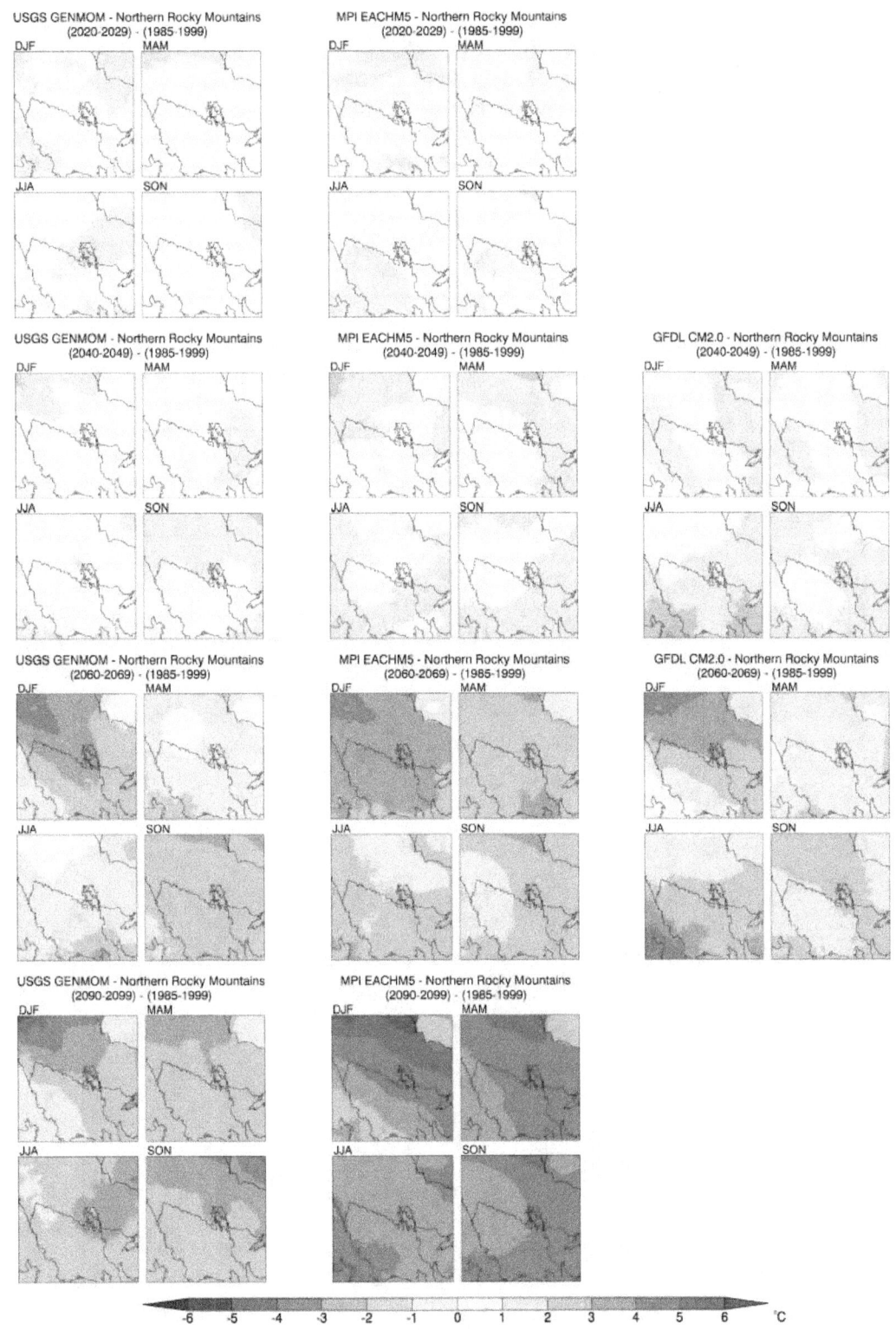

Figure 19. Differences between seasonal average 2-m air temperature climatologies for future decades (2020–2029, 2040–2049, 2060–2069, and 2090–2099) versus 1985–1999 over the NRM domain for the three RegCM3 projections. Column 1: GMA2, column 2: ECH5, and column 3: GFDL. Row 1: 2020–2029, row 2: 2040–2049, row 3: 2060–2069, and row 4: 2090–2099.

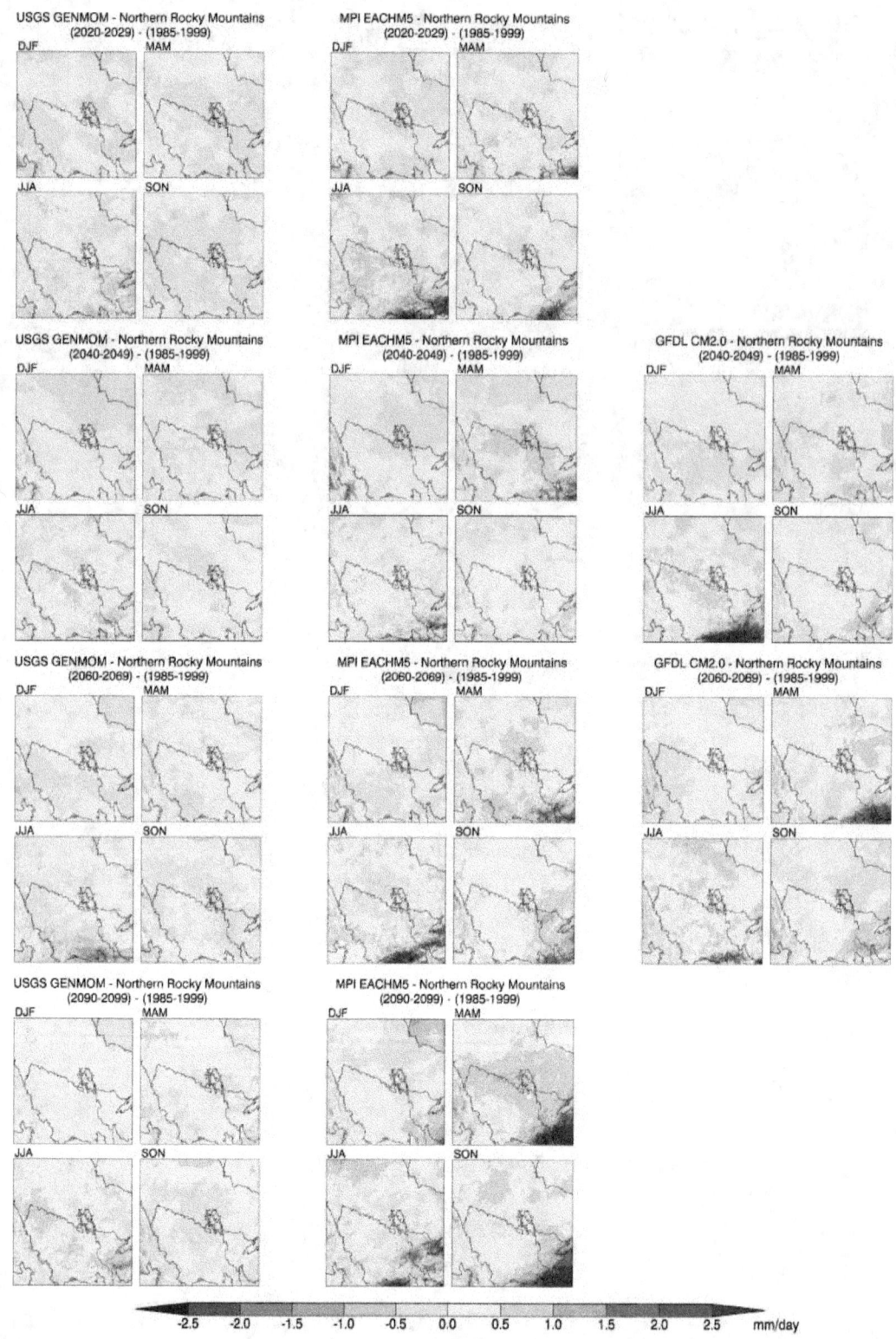

Figure 20. Differences between seasonal average precipitation climatologies for future decades (2020–2029, 2040–2049, 2060–2069, and 2090–2099) versus 1985–1999 over the NRM domain for the three RegCM3 projections. Column 1: GMA2, column 2: ECH5, and column 3: GFDL. Row 1: 2020–2029, row 2: 2040–2049, row 3: 2060–2069, and row 4: 2090–2099.

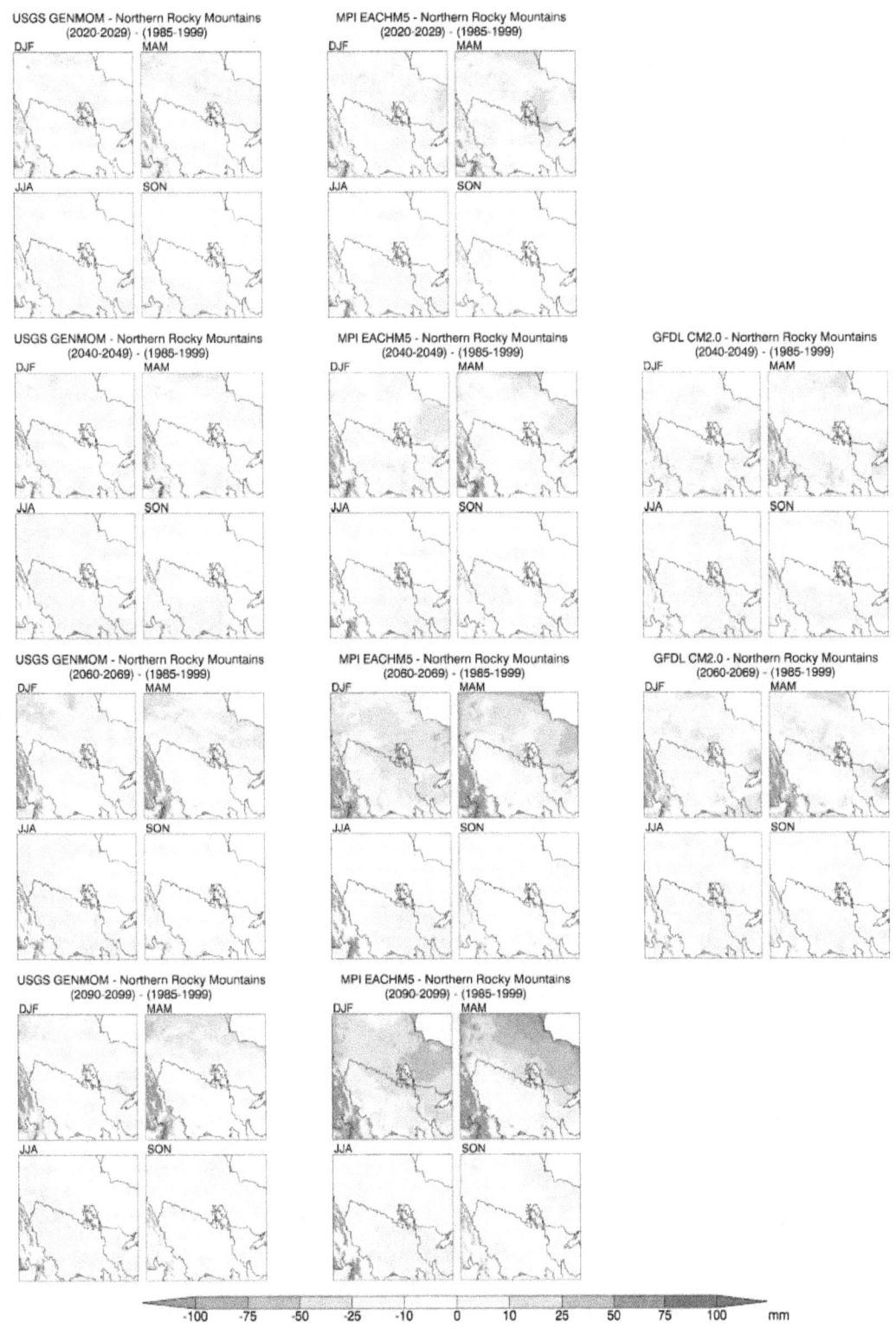

Figure 21. Differences between seasonal average snow water equivalent climatologies for future decades (2020–2029, 2040–2049, 2060–2069, and 2090–2099) versus 1985–1999 over the NRM domain for the three RegCM3 projections. Column 1: GMA2, column 2: ECH5 and column 3: GFDL. Row 1: 2020–2029, row 2: 2040–2049, row 3: 2060–2069, and row 4: 2090–2099.

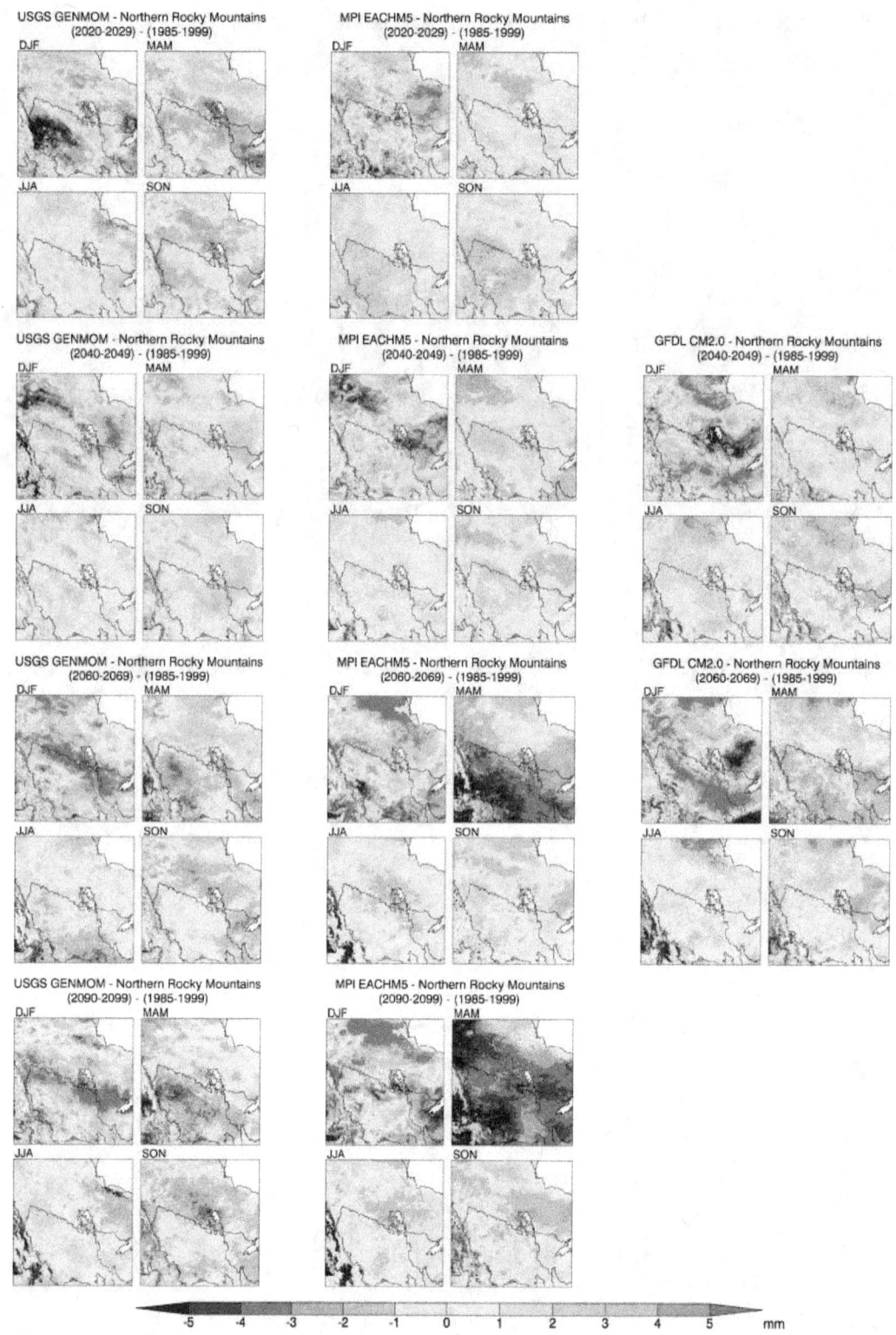

Figure 22. Differences between seasonal average root-zone soil moisture climatologies for future decades (2020–2029, 2040–2049, 2060–2069, and 2090–2099) versus 1985–1999 over the NRM domain for the three RegCM3 projections. Column 1: GMA2, column 2: ECH5, and column 3: GFDL. Row 1: 2020–2029, row 2: 2040–2049, row 3: 2060–2069, and row 4: 2090–2099.

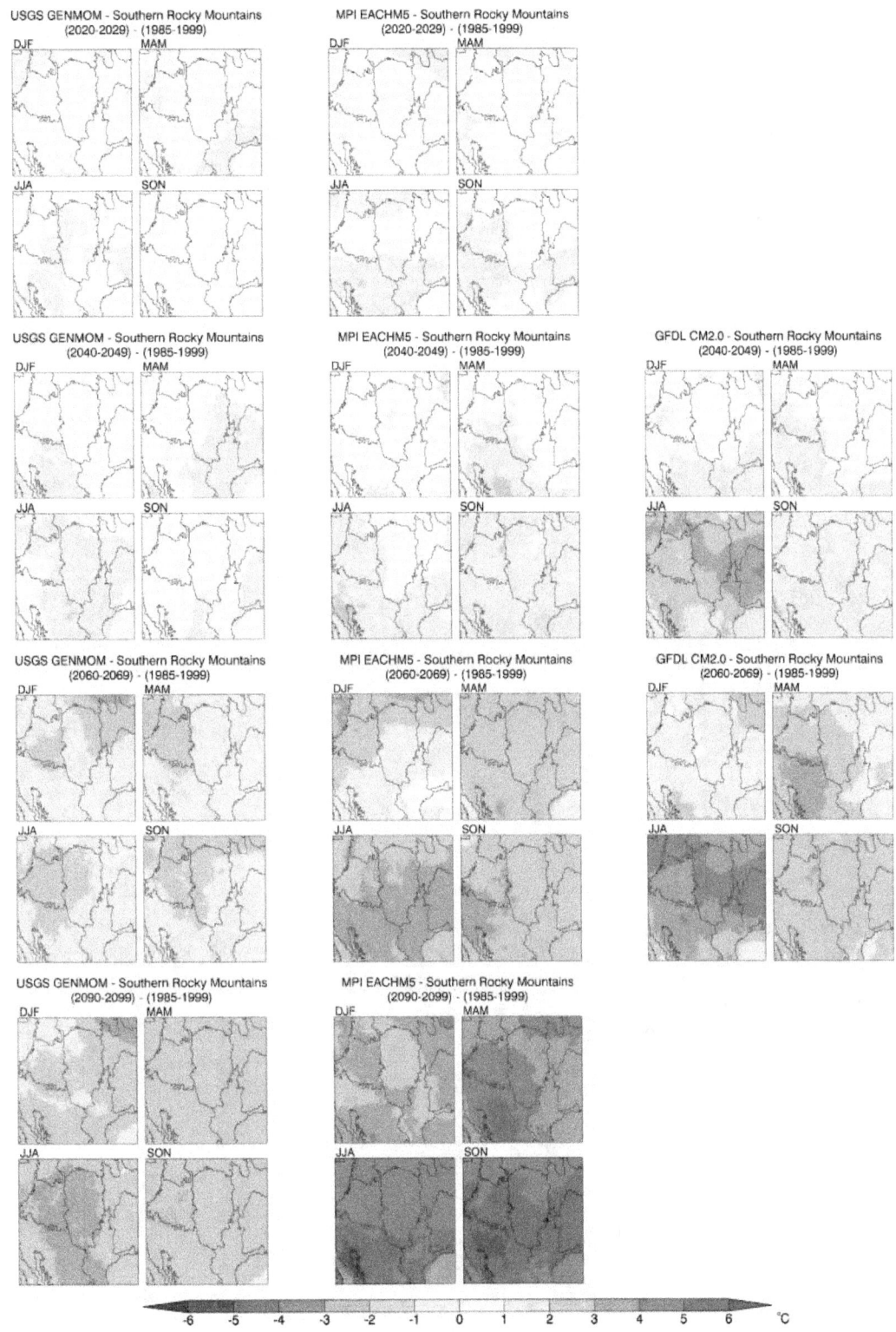

Figure 23. Differences between seasonal average 2-m air temperature climatologies for future decades (2020–2029, 2040–2049, 2060–2069, and 2090–2099) versus 1985–1999 over the SRM domain for the three RegCM3 projections. Column 1: GMA2, column 2: ECH5, and column 3: GFDL. Row 1: 2020–2029, row 2: 2040–2049, row 3: 2060–2069, and row 4: 2090–2099.

45

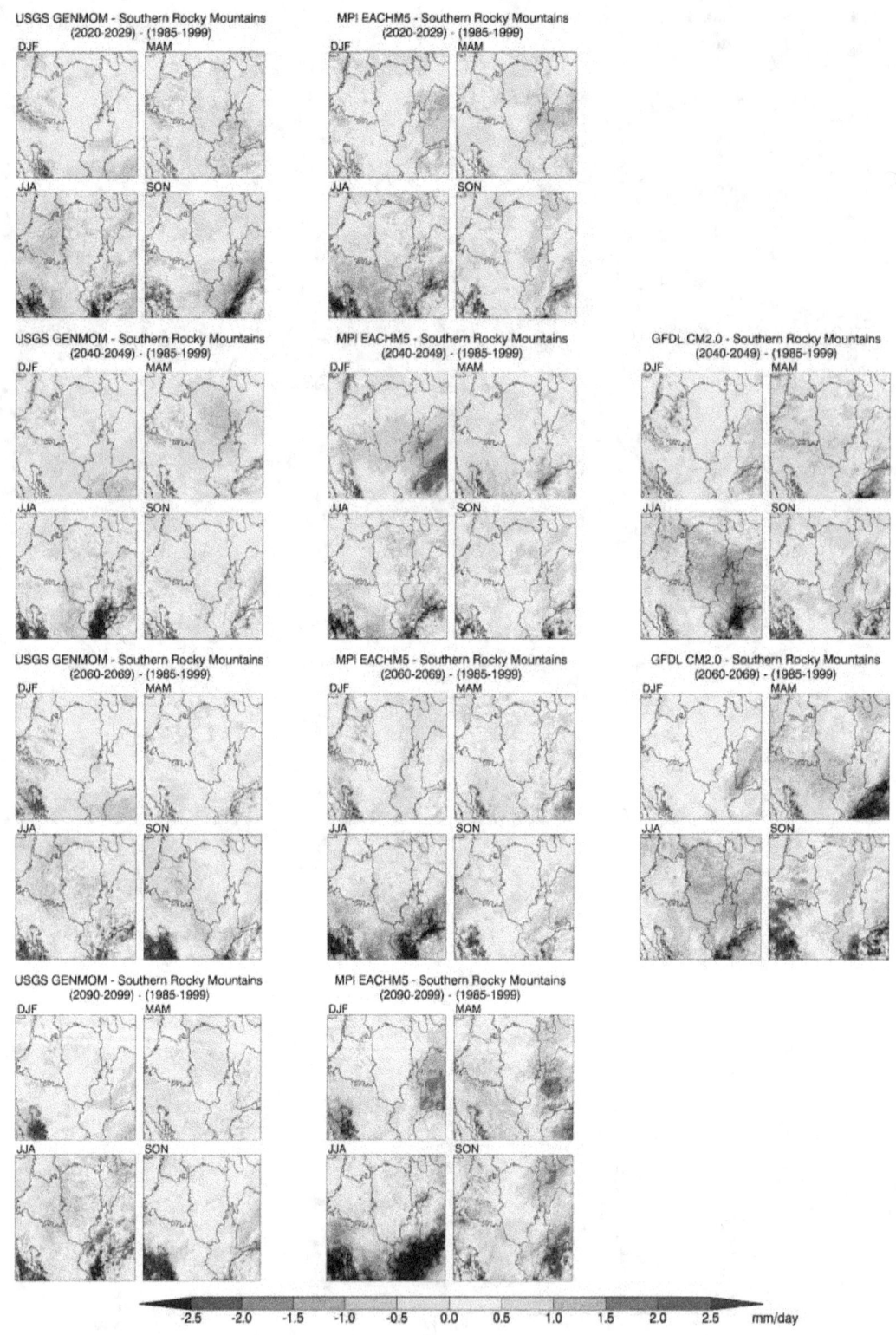

Figure 24. Differences between seasonal average precipitation climatologies for future decades (2020–2029, 2040–2049, 2060–2069, and 2090–2099) versus 1985–1999 over the SRM domain for the three RegCM3 projections. Column 1: GMA2, column 2: ECH5, and column 3: GFDL. Row 1: 2020–2029, row 2: 2040–2049, row 3: 2060–2069, and row 4: 2090–2099.

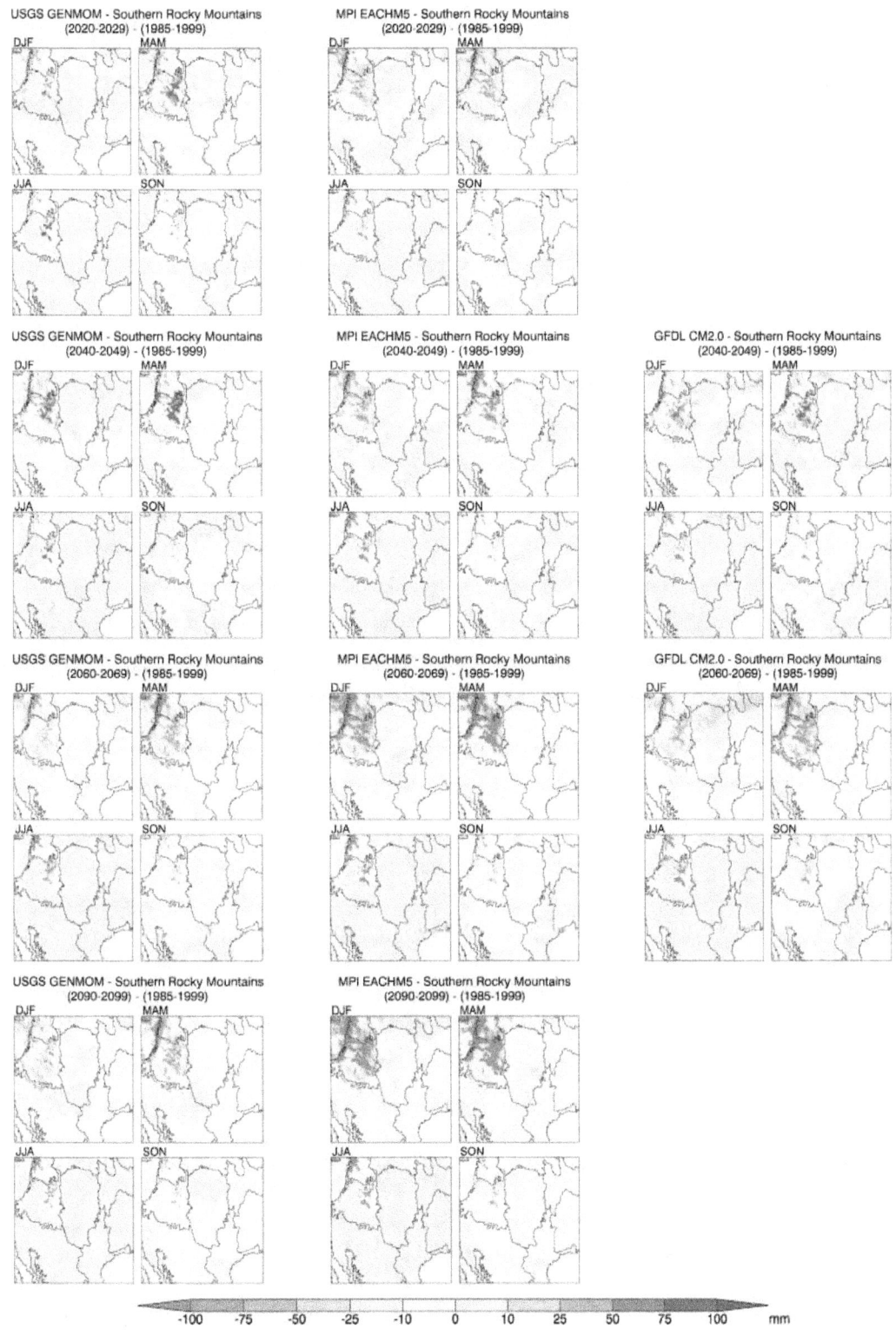

Figure 25. Differences between seasonal average snow water equivalent climatologies for future decades (2020–2029, 2040–2049, 2060–2069, and 2090–2099) versus 1985–1999 over the SRM domain for the three RegCM3 projections. Column 1: GMA2, column 2: ECH5, and column 3: GFDL. Row 1: 2020–2029, row 2: 2040–2049, row 3: 2060–2069, and row 4: 2090–2099.

47

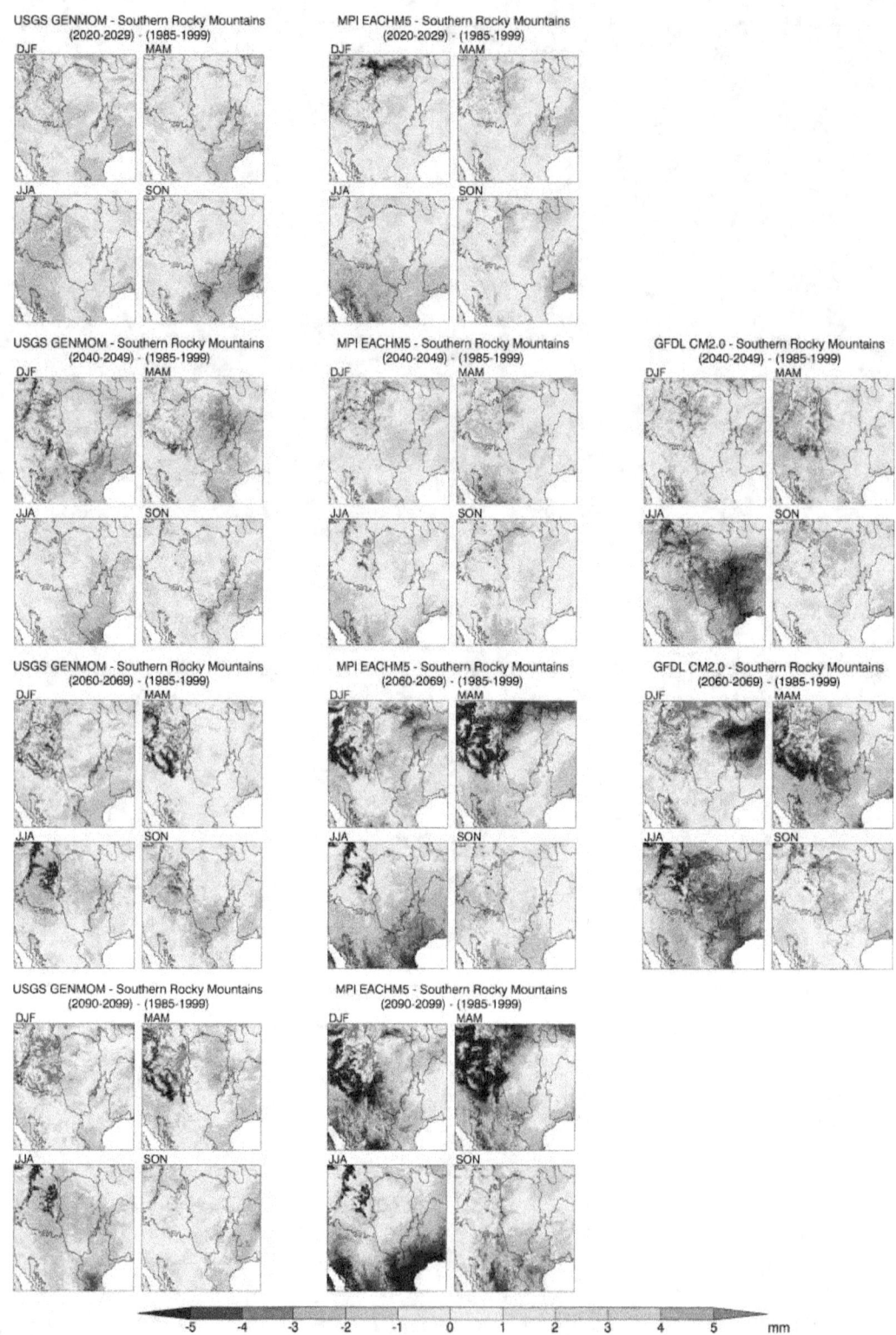

Figure 26. Differences between seasonal average root-zone soil moisture climatologies for future decades (2020–2029, 2040–2049, 2060–2069, and 2090–2099) versus 1985–1999 over the SRM domain for the three RegCM3 projections. Column 1: GMA2, column 2: ECH5, and column 3: GFDL. Row 1: 2020–2029, row 2: 2040–2049, row 3: 2060–2069, and row 4: 2090–2099.

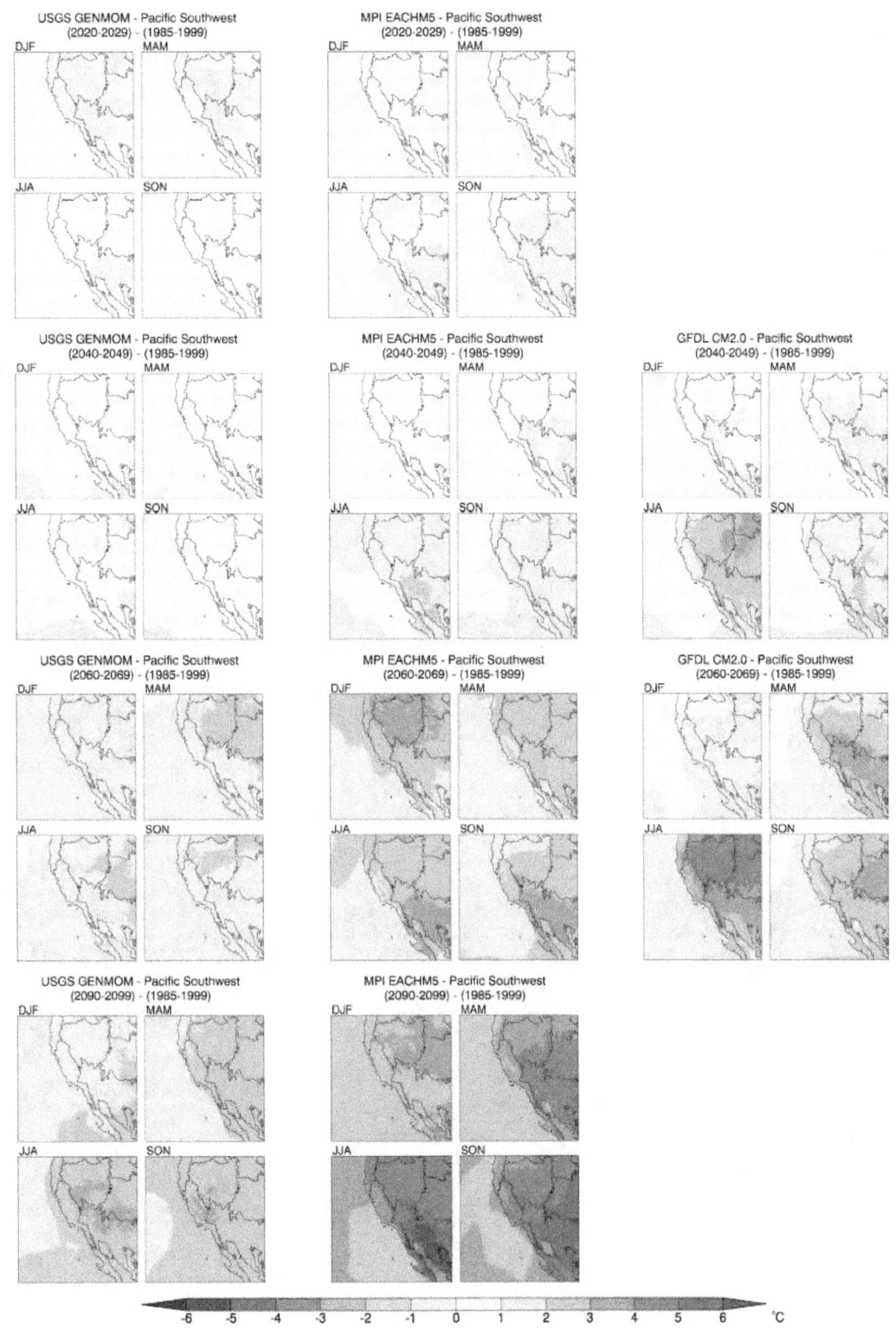

Figure 27. Differences between seasonal average 2-m air temperature climatologies for future decades (2020–2029, 2040–2049, 2060–2069, and 2090–2099) versus 1985–1999 over the PSW domain for the three RegCM3 projections. Column 1: GMA2, column 2: ECH5, and column 3: GFDL. Row 1: 2020–2029, row 2: 2040–2049, row 3: 2060–2069, and row 4: 2090–2099.

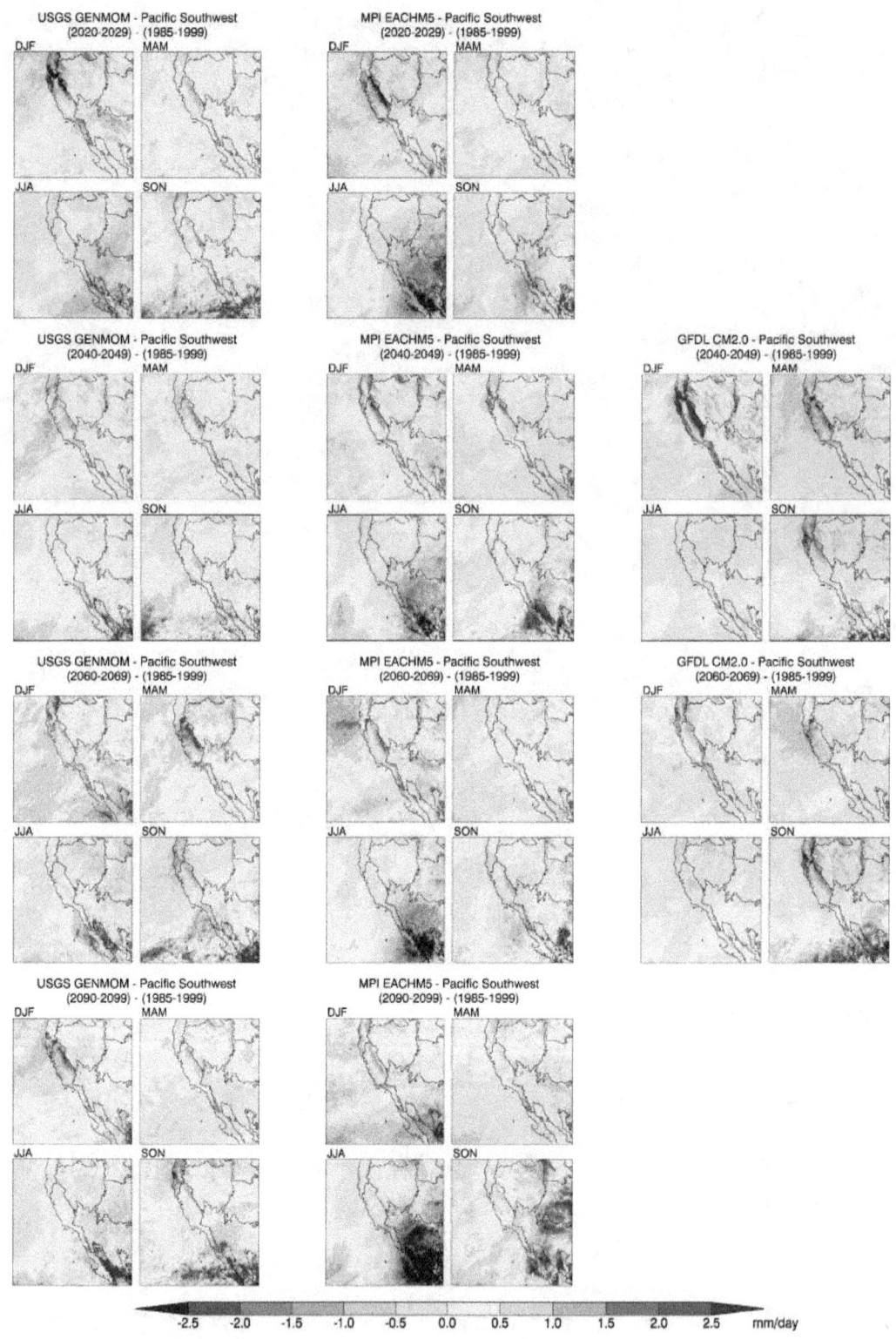

Figure 28. Differences between seasonal average precipitation climatologies for future decades (2020–2029, 2040–2049, 2060–2069, and 2090–2099) versus 1985–1999 over the PSW domain for the three RegCM3 projections. Column 1: GMA2, column 2: ECH5, and column 3: GFDL. Row 1: 2020–2029, row 2: 2040–2049, row 3: 2060–2069, and row 4: 2090–2099.

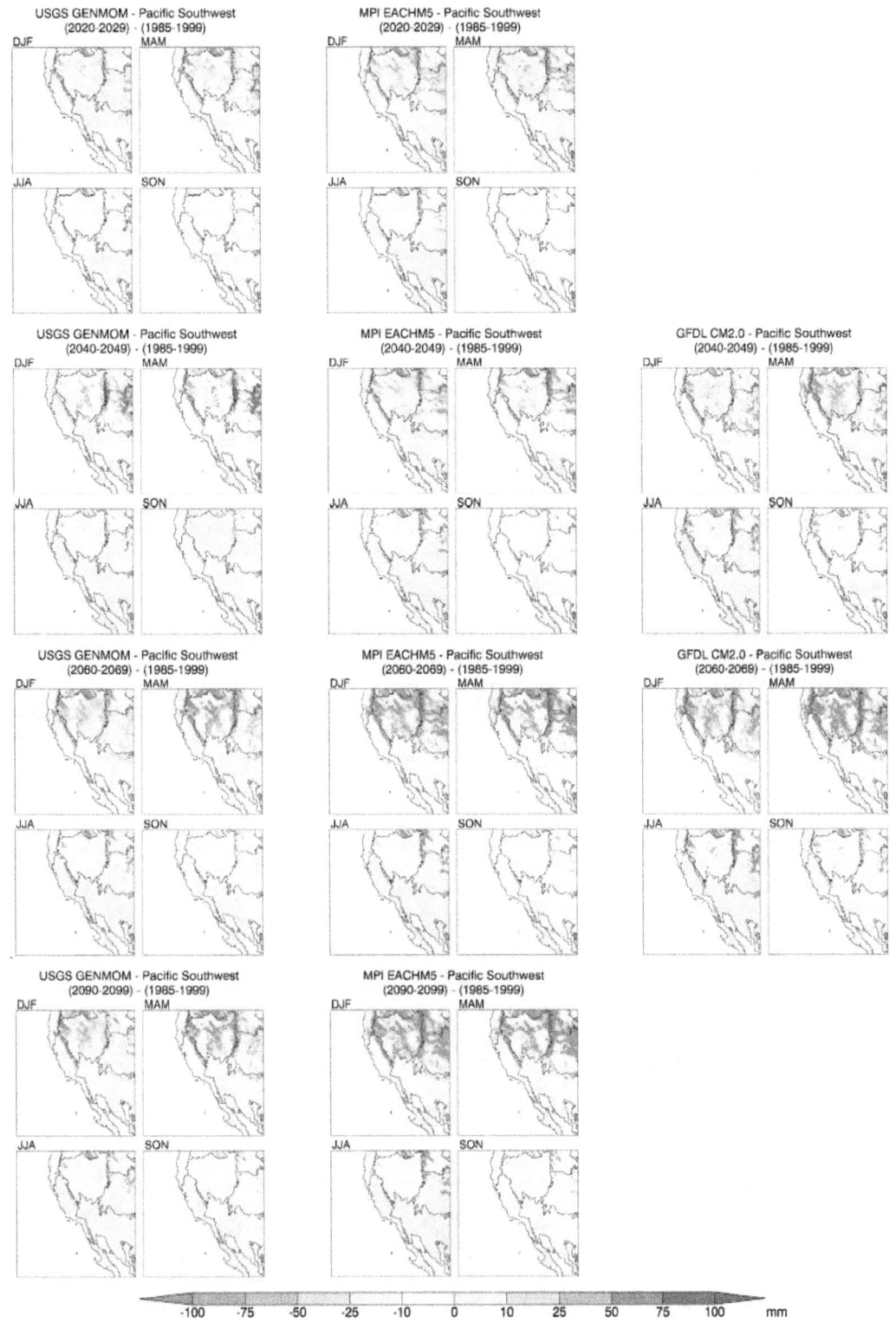

Figure 29. Differences between seasonal average snow water equivalent climatologies for future decades (2020–2029, 2040–2049, 2060–2069, and 2090–2099) versus 1985–1999 over the PSW domain for the three RegCM3 projections. Column 1: GMA2, column 2: ECH5, and column 3: GFDL. Row 1: 2020–2029, row 2: 2040–2049, row 3: 2060–2069, and row 4: 2090–2099.

51

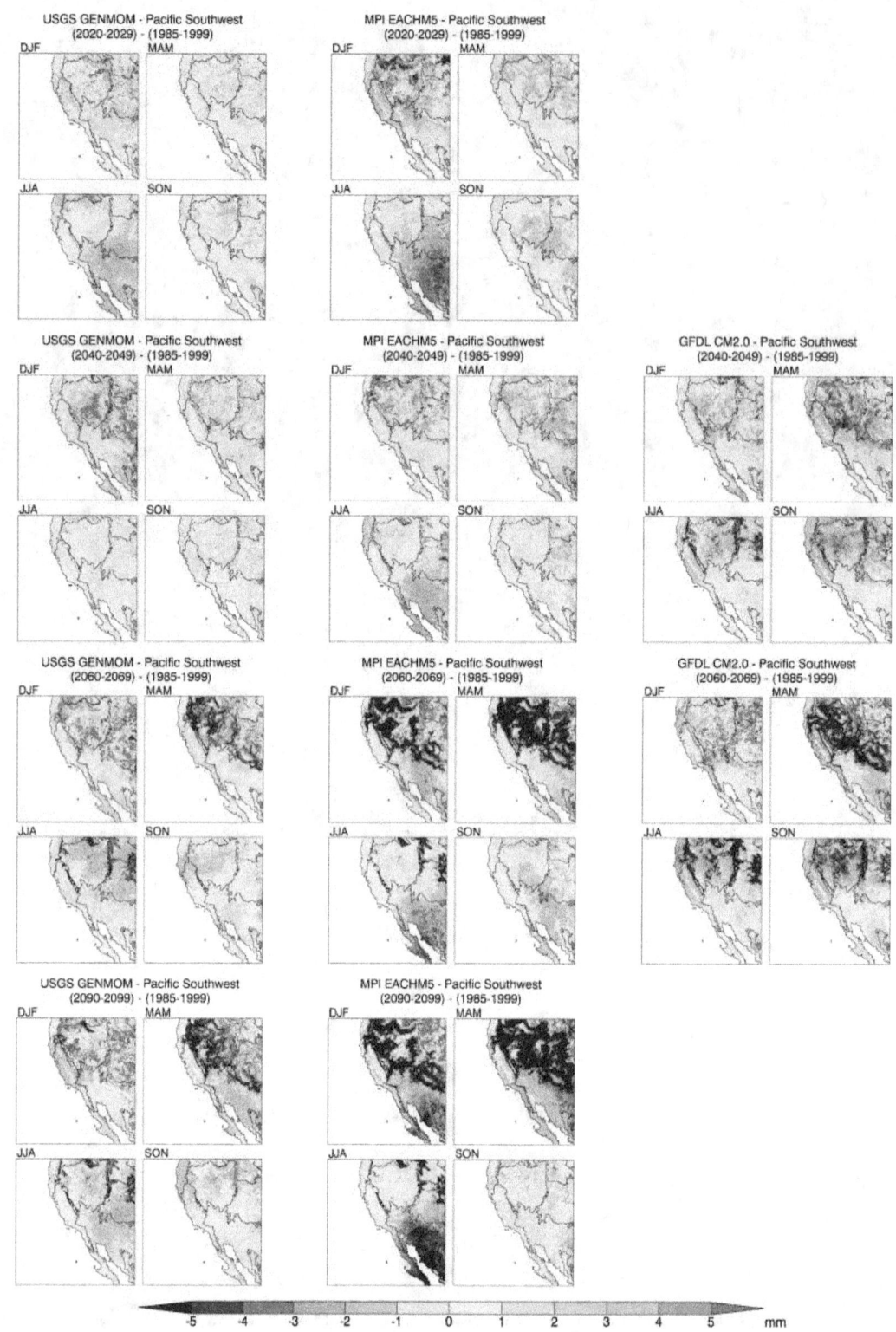

Figure 30. Differences between seasonal average root-zone soil moisture climatologies for future decades (2020–2029, 2040–2049, 2060–2069, and 2090–2099) versus 1985–1999 over the PSW domain for the three RegCM3 projections. Column 1: GMA2, column 2: ECH5, and column 3: GFDL. Row 1: 2020–2029, row 2: 2040–2049, row 3: 2060–2069, and row 4: 2090–2099.

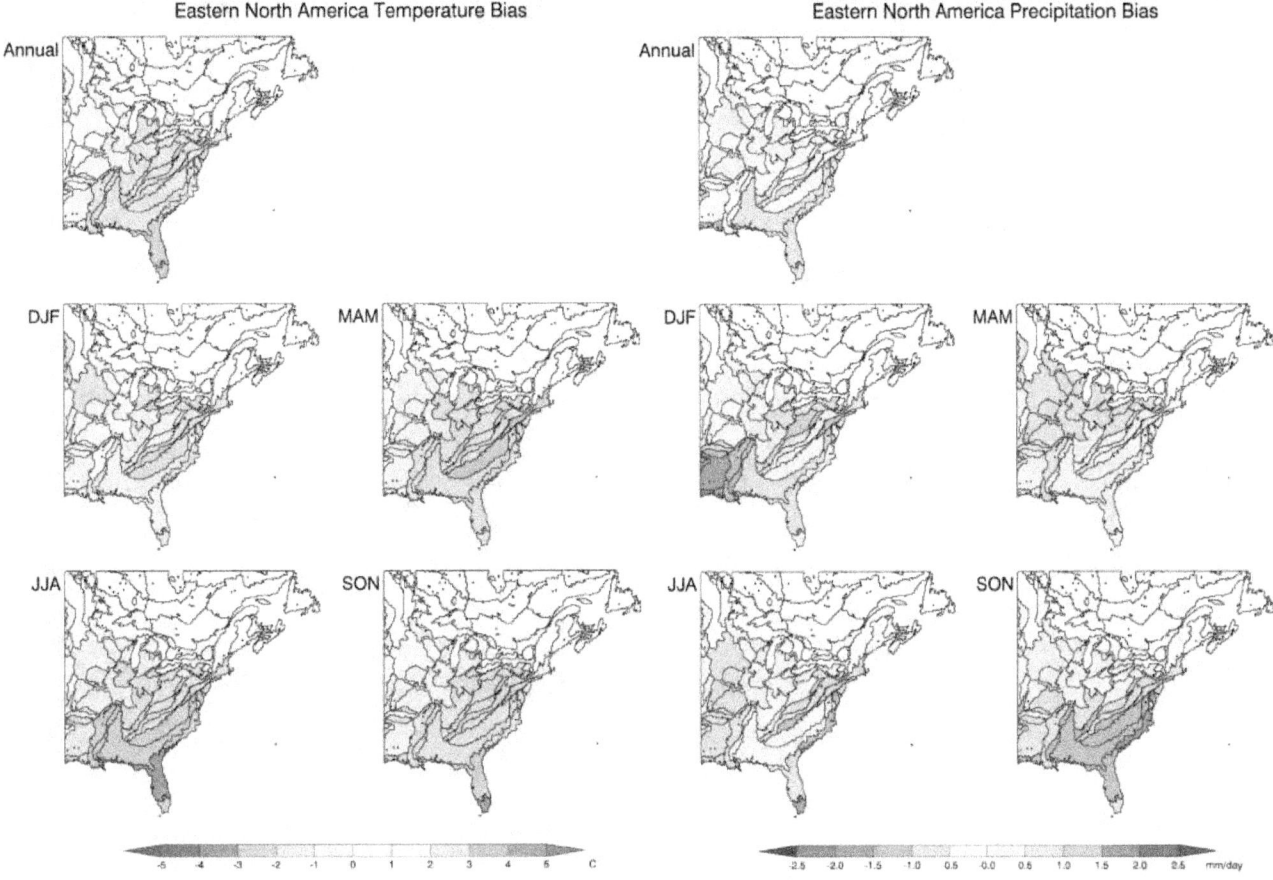

Figure 31. Annual and seasonal differences (biases) between simulated 2-m air temperatures (left) and precipitation rates (right) and PRISM values averaged over the EPA Level III ecoregions for the ENA domain. The averaging period is 1985–1999. PRISM data from Daly and others (1994).

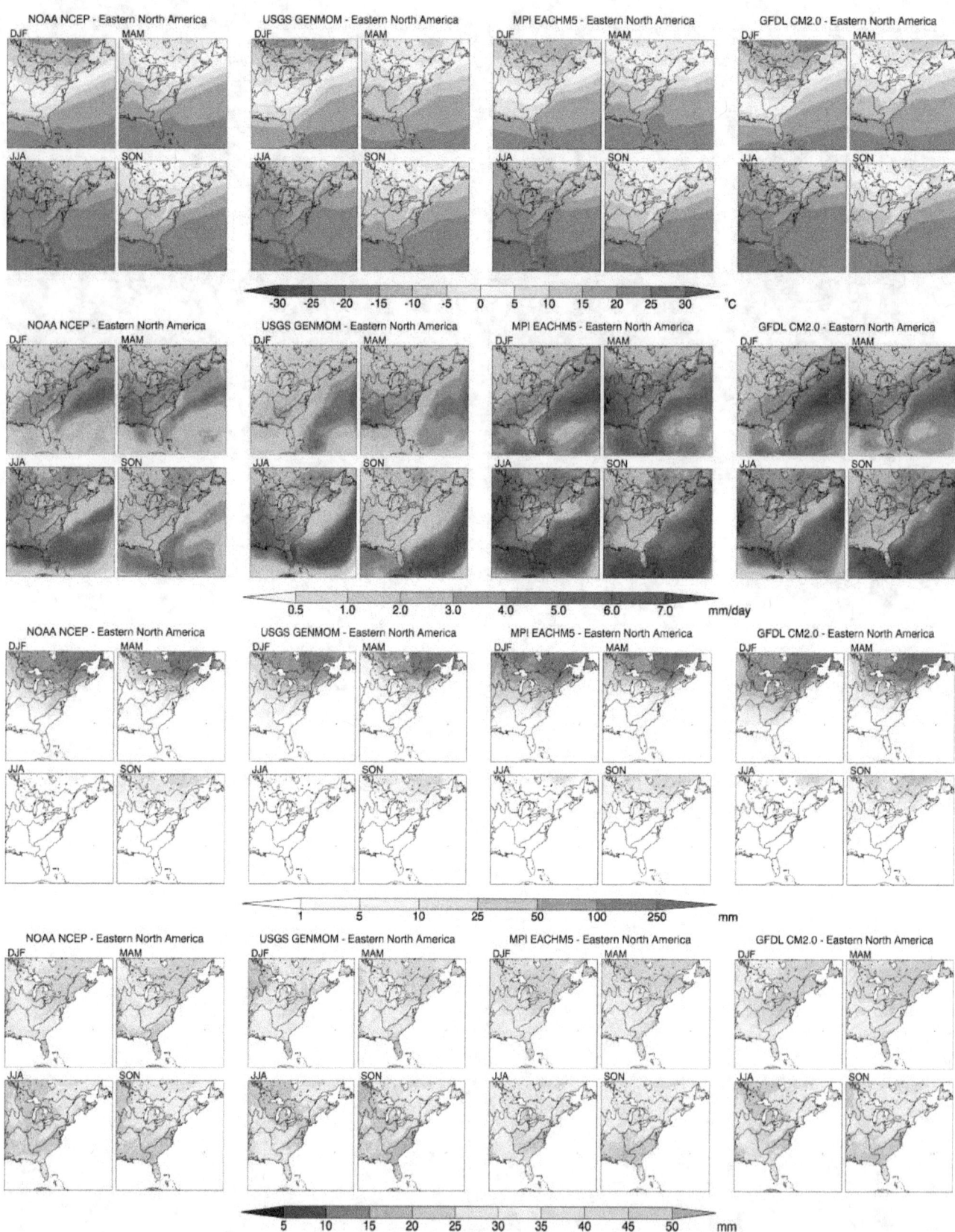

Figure 32. Seasonal average climatologies (averaging period is 1985–1999) over the ENA domain for the four RegCM3 simulations. Row 1: 2 m air temperature, row 2: precipitation rate, row 3: snow-water equivalent, and row 4: root-zone soil moisture.

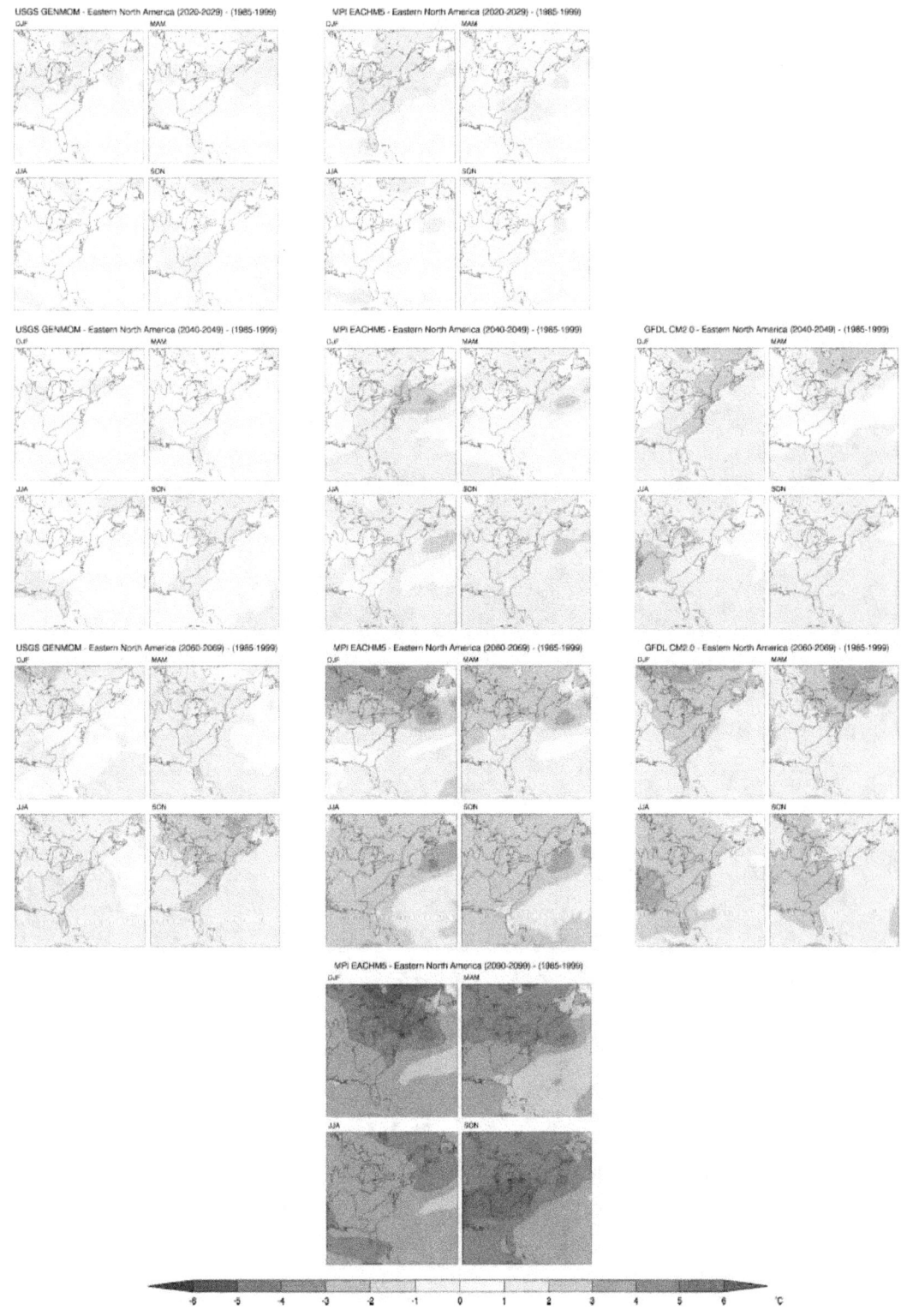

Figure 33. Differences between seasonal average 2-m air temperature climatologies for future decades (2020–2029, 2040–2049, 2060–2069, and 2090–2099) versus 1985–1999 over the ENA domain for the three RegCM3 projections. Column 1: GMA2, column 2: ECH5, and column 3: GFDL. Row 1: 2020–2029, row 2: 2040–2049, row 3: 2060–2069, and row 4: 2090–2099.

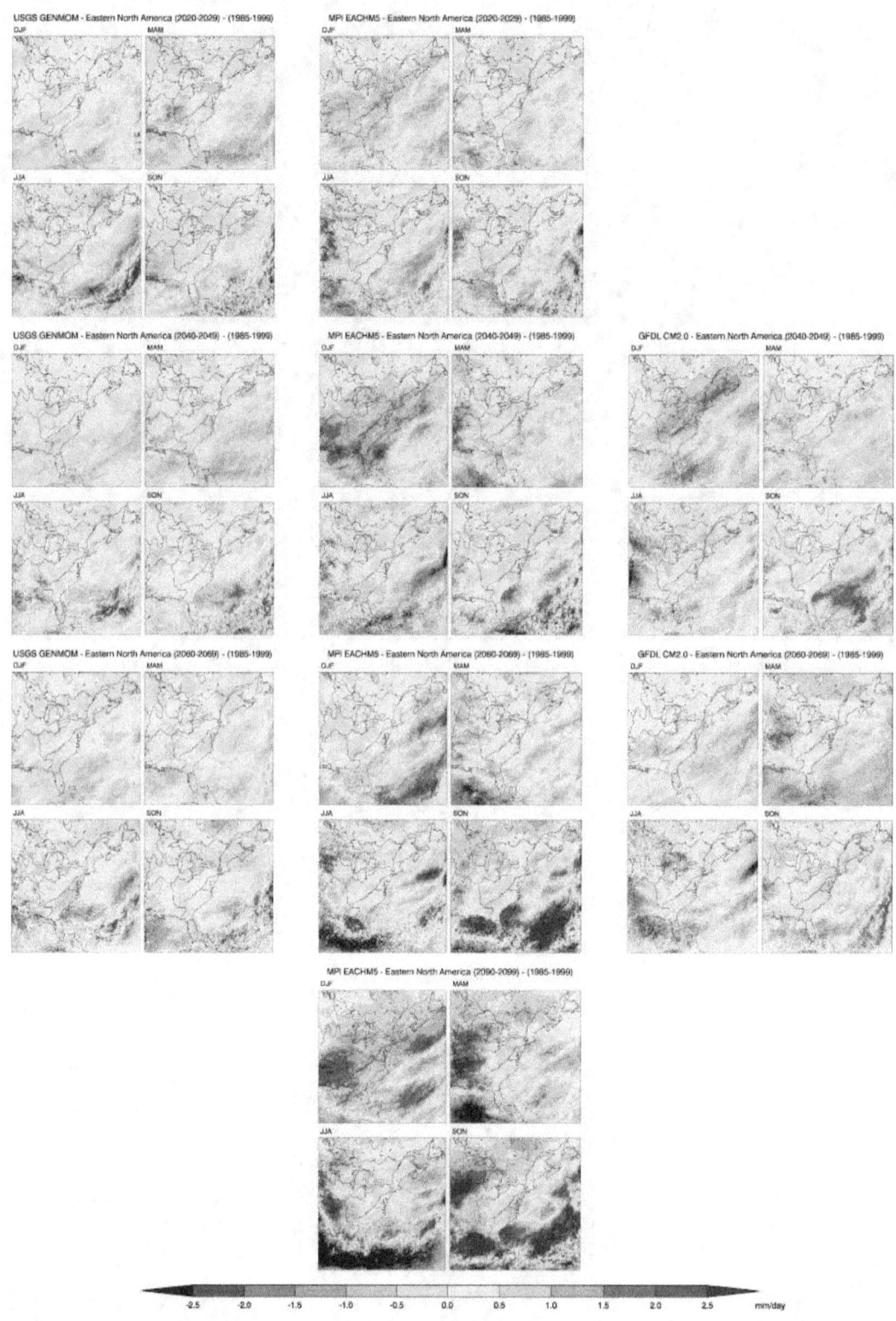

Figure 34. Differences between seasonal average precipitation climatologies for future decades (2020–2029, 2040–2049, 2060–2069, and 2090–2099) versus 1985–1999 over the ENA domain for the three RegCM3 projections. Column 1: GMA2, column 2: ECH5, and column 3: GFDL. Row 1: 2020–2029, row 2: 2040–2049, row 3: 2060–2069, and row 4: 2090–2099.

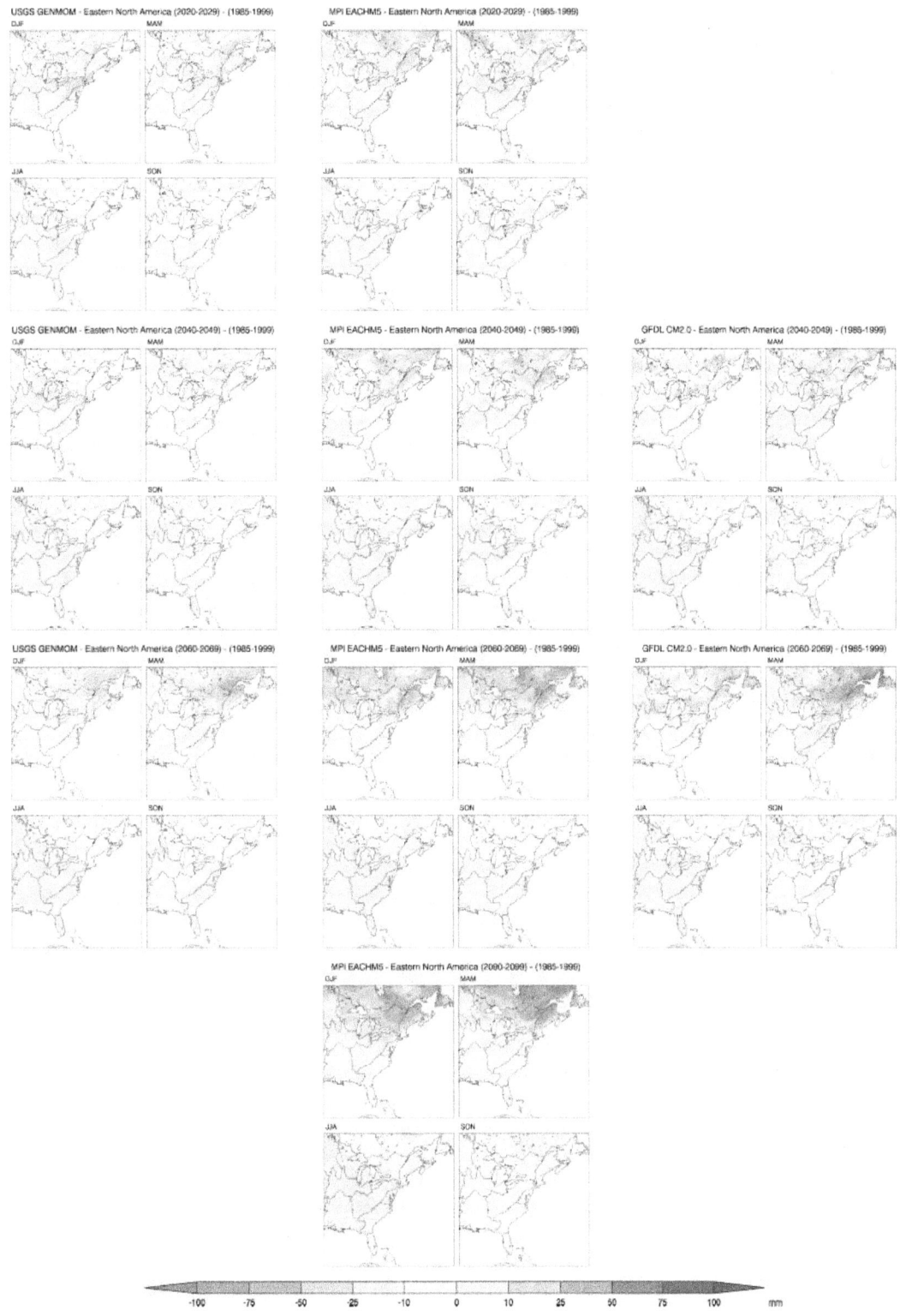

Figure 35. Differences between seasonal average snow water equivalent climatologies for future decades (2020–2029, 2040–2049, 2060–2069, and 2090–2099) versus 1985–1999 over the ENA domain for the three RegCM3 projections. Column 1: GMA2, column 2: ECH5, and column 3: GFDL. Row 1: 2020–2029, row 2: 2040–2049, row 3: 2060–2069, and row 4: 2090–2099.

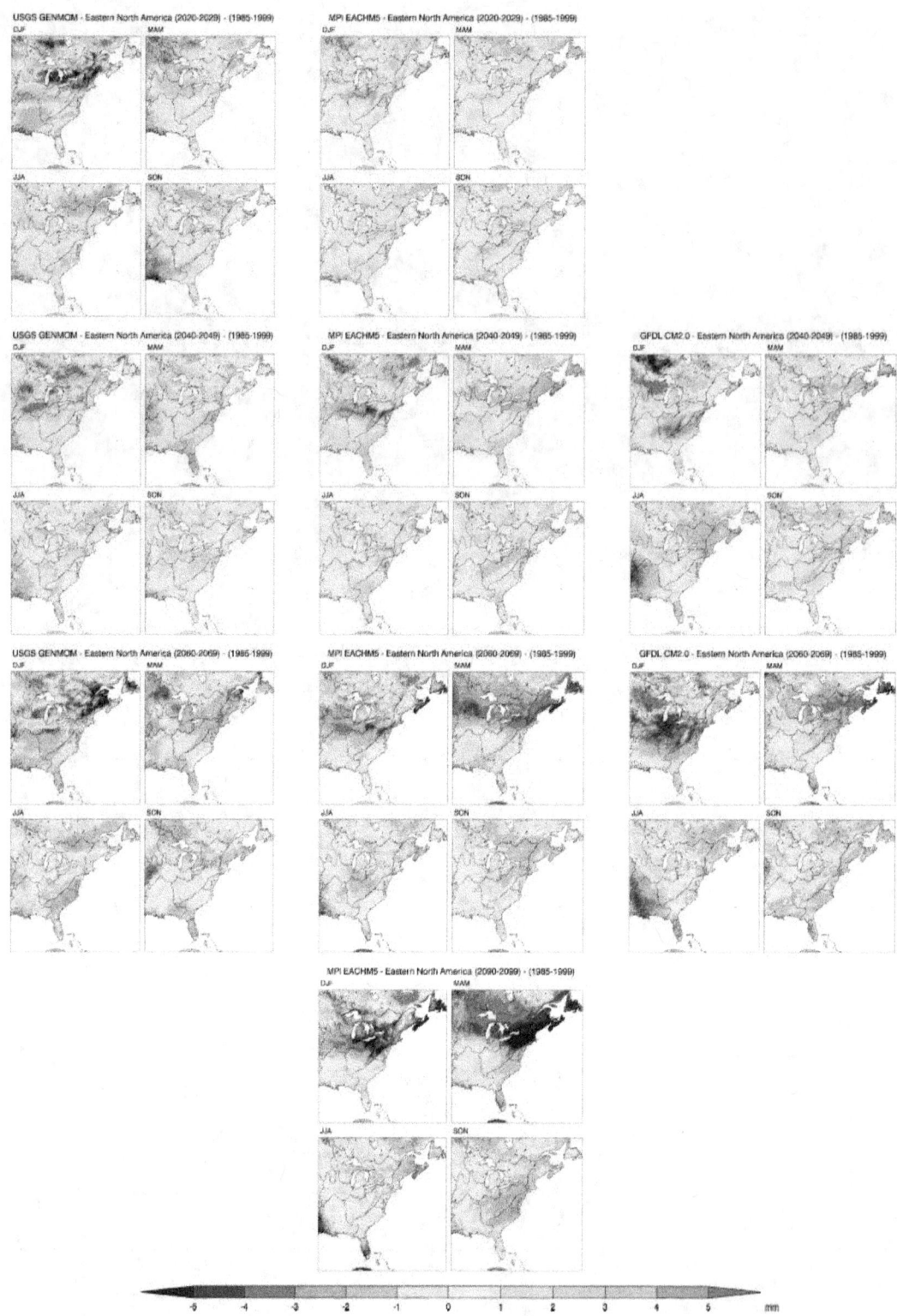

Figure 36. Differences between seasonal average root-zone soil moisture climatologies for future decades (2020–2029, 2040–2049, 2060–2069, and 2090–2099) versus 1985–1999 over the ENA domain for the three RegCM3 projections. Column 1: GMA2, column 2: ECH5, and column 3: GFDL. Row 1: 2020–2029, row 2: 2040–2049, row 3: 2060–2069, and row 4: 2090–2099.

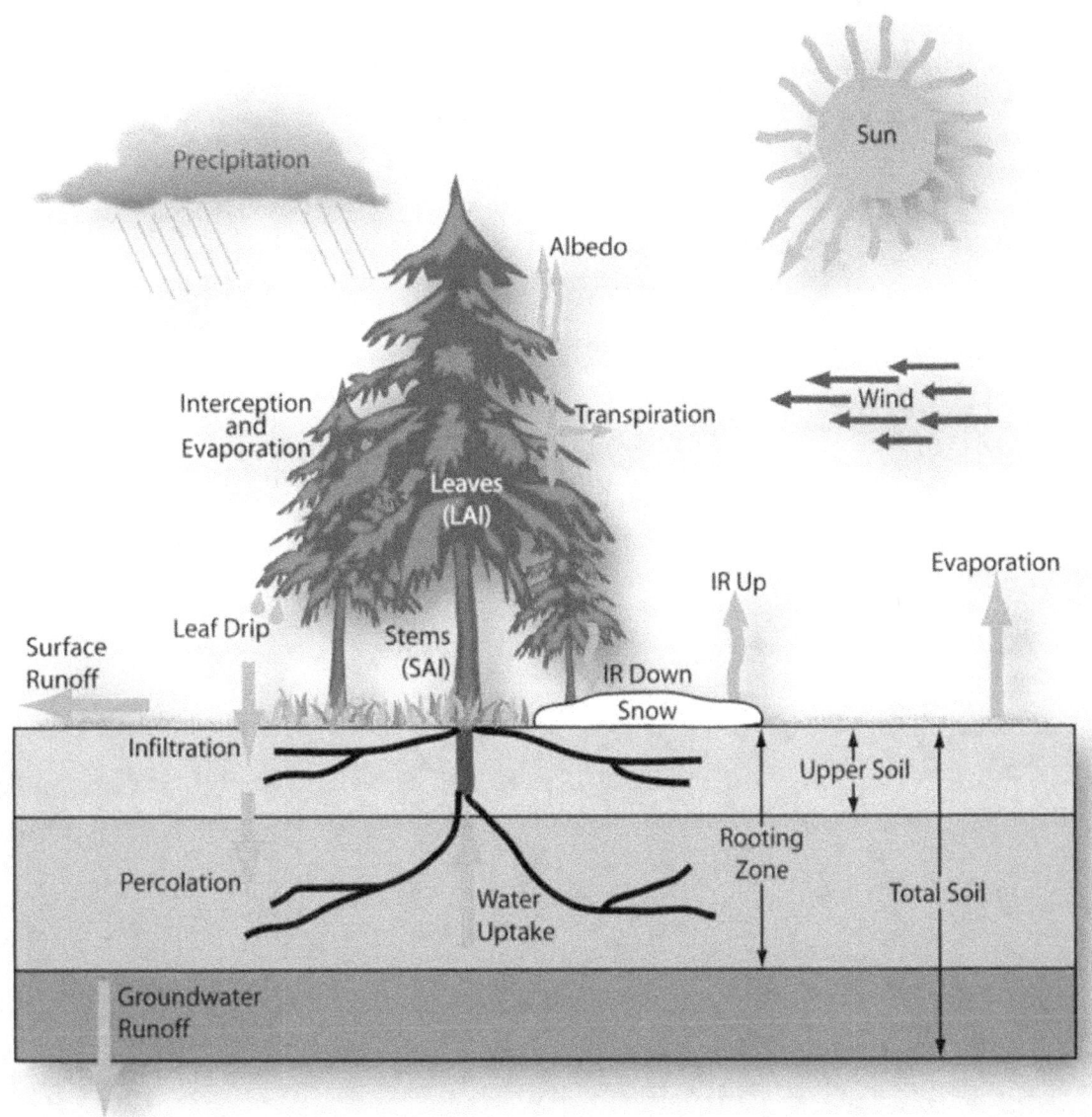

Figure 37. Diagram of the BATS surface physics model and processes represented, as implemented in RegCM3.

Table 1. Selected examples of the key advantages and disadvantages of downscaling techniques.

Statistical	Dynamical
+ fast (relatively)	+ true simulation of high resolution forcing and climate
+ high resolution (e.g., 4 km or less)	+ large, internally consistent set of atmospheric and surface variables
+ multiple GCMs for ensembles and different emissions scenarios	- time consuming
- limited ability to correct for displaced features such as mountain ranges	- limited number of GCMs
- may not conserve mass and heat	- added model biases

Table 2. Information for the GCMs used to drive the RegCM3 simulations.

GCM	RegCM3 Naming	Modeling Center	Atmosphere Resolution	Ocean Resolution
NOAA-NCEP (NCEP-DOE Reanalysis I and II)	NCEP	U.S. Department of Commerce/National Oceanic and Atmospheric Administration, USA	T62 (~2.8° × 2.8°)	1.75° × 1.75° L31
GFDL CM 2.0	GFDL	U.S. Department of Commerce/National Oceanic and Atmospheric Administration (NOAA)/Geophysical Fluid Dynamics Laboratory (GFDL), USA	2.0° × 2.5° L24	0.3°–1.0° × 1.0°
MPI ECHAM5	ECH5	Max Planck Institute for Meteorology, Germany	T63 (~1.9° × 1.9°) L31	1.5° × 1.5° L40
GENMOM	GMA2	Penn State University, USGS/Oregon State University	T31 (~3.75° × 3.75°)	T31 (~3.75° × 3.75°)

Table 3. Time periods covered by the 50-km North America and 15-km RegCM Western North America and Eastern North America simulations.

Driving GCM	North America	West	East
NCEP Reanalysis	1968-2010	1968-2010	1982-2007
MPI ECHAM5 (20C, A2)	1968-1999 2010-2099	1968-1999 2010-2099	1968-1999 2020-2099
GFDL CM2.0 (20C, A2)	1968-1999 2038-2069	1968-1999 2038-2069	1968-1999 2038-2069
PSU/USGS GENMOM (A2)	1968-1999 2010-2099	1968-1999 2010-2099	1980-1999 2020-2080

Table 4. BATS surface types (listed below) and their associated physical properties in the RegCM3.

Parameter	\\ Land cover/Vegetation type																		
	1	2	3	4	5	6	7	8	9	10	11	12	13	14	15	16	17	18	19
Max fractional vegetation cover	0.85	0.80	0.80	0.80	0.80	0.90	0.00	0.00	0.60	0.85	0.35	0.00	0.80	0.00	0.00	0.80	0.80	0.80	0.80
Difference between max fractional cover and cover at 269 K	0.6	0.1	0.1	0.1	0.5	0.3	0.0	0.0	0.2	0.6	0.0	0.4	0.0	0.0	0.2	0.3	0.2	0.4	0.4
Roughness length (m)	0.08	0.05	1.00	1.00	0.80	2.00	2.00	0.10	0.05	0.04	0.06	0.10	0.01	0.0004	0.0004	0.10	0.10	0.80	0.30
Displacement height (m)	0.0	0.0	9.0	9.0	0.0	18.0	0.0	0.0	0.0	0.0	0.0	0.0	0.0	0.0	0.0	0.0	0.0	0.0	0.0
Min stomatal resistance (s/m)	45	60	80	80	120	60	60	200	80	45	150	200	45	200	200	80	80	100	120
Max Leaf Area Index	6	2	6	6	6	6	6	0	0	6	6	0	6	0	0	6	6	6	6
Min Leaf Area Index	0.5	0.5	5.0	1.0	1.0	5.0	0.5	0.0	0.0	0.5	0.5	0.0	0.5	0.0	0.0	5.0	1.0	3.0	0.5
Stem (dead matter) Index	0.5	4.0	2.0	2.0	2.0	2.0	2.0	0.5	0.5	2.0	2.0	2.0	2.0	2.0	2.0	2.0	2.0	2.0	2.0
Inverse square root of leaf dimension ($m^{1/2}$)	10	5	5	5	5	5	5	5	5	5	5	5	5	5	5	5	5	5	5
Light sensitivity factor ($m^2 W^{-1}$)	0.02	0.02	0.06	0.06	0.06	0.06	0.02	0.02	0.02	0.02	0.02	0.02	0.02	0.02	0.02	0.02	0.02	0.06	0.02
Upper soil layer depth (mm)	100	100	100	100	100	100	100	100	100	100	100	100	100	100	100	100	100	100	100
Root zone soil depth (mm)	1500	1500	1500	1500	1500	1500	1500	1500	1500	1500	1500	1500	1500	1500	1500	1500	1500	1500	1500
Total soil depth (mm)	3000	3000	3000	3000	3000	3000	3000	3000	3000	3000	3000	3000	3000	3000	3000	3000	3000	3000	3000
Soil texture type	6	6	6	6	7	6	6	6	3	6	5	12	6	6	6	6	5	6	6
Soil color type	5	3	4	4	4	4	4	4	3	3	2	1	5	5	5	5	3	4	6
Vegetation albedo for wavelengths < 0.7 um	0.01	0.05	0.05	0.05	0.08	0.08	0.04	0.08	0.20	0.20	0.08	0.80	0.06	0.07	0.07	0.07	0.05	0.06	0.06
Vegetation albedo for wavelengths > 0.7 um	0.30	0.30	0.23	0.23	0.28	0.20	0.20	0.30	0.40	0.30	0.28	0.60	0.18	0.30	0.30	0.23	0.28	0.24	0.18

1. Crop/mixed farming
2. Short grass
3. Evergreen needleleaf tree
4. Deciduous needleleaf tree
5. Deciduous broadleaf tree
6. Evergreen broadleaf tree
7. Tall grass
8. Desert
9. Tundra
10. Irrigated Crop
11. Semi-desert
12. Ice cap/glacier
13. Bog or marsh
14. Inland water
15. Ocean
16. Evergreen shrub
17. Deciduous shrub
18. Mixed Woodland
19. Forest/Field mosaic
20. Water and Land mixture